W9-BXX-039

"Wise, thoughtful, compassionate, insightful and, above all, practical, this brief book will help you confront those 'little sins' that nonetheless have a very big effect on your Christian life."
— James Martin, S.J., author of *Jesus: A Pilgrimage*

"Elizabeth Scalsia takes a wry and insightful look at how modern Catholics can make an effective examination of conscience, recognizing not only their faults but also the mercy of forgiveness. Pope Francis has urged Catholics not to be afraid or ashamed to go to confession. This book is the perfect companion for those making that journey."
— John Thavis, author of *The Vatican Diaries* and *The Vatican Prophecies*

"The Internet's 'Anchoress' cautions us to limit our time on social media in this book! Is it a miracle? Decide for yourself, dear reader. Read this book and God may just work miracles in your life too, giving you the desire — and the graces — to eradicate the little sins in your life so that you can get on with the business of being Christian, already! Jesus invites and demands radical conversion. This book is an accessible, practical guide to repentance, drenched in Divine Mercy."
— Kathryn Jean Lopez, editor-at-large of National Review Online

"Captivating, witty, and wise, *Little Sins* is a big gift of heart and hope. What may be most audacious: Elizabeth Scalia finds a way to share some of her own story and make it ours too. In this book, the woman countless readers know as 'The Anchoress' takes off her veil, lets down her hair, and reveals . . . us. Anyone who wants a deeper understanding of what makes us poor sinners do what we do, and who yearns to grow, will find in this book a delightful and helpful guide. You might just read it and weep — with gratitude."
— Deacon Greg Kandra, Diocese of Brooklyn, blogger at Aleteia.org

"No one knew better than Christ that murder, adultery, and the pillaging of the planet begin with the 'small' sins of anger, petty jealousy, and resentment. No one knew better how very much we love to point the finger at our neighbor and how very much we resist examining our own consciences. No one knew better that the point isn't so much to be 'good' as to open ourselves to receive the priceless gift of one another — in all our brokenness and all our glory. Like St. Thérèse of Lisieux, Elizabeth Scalia has penetrated to the heart of the Gospels."

— Heather King, author of *Stripped: At the Intersection of Cancer, Culture, and Christ*

"From gossip to gluttony and all points between, vice and sin wreak havoc on our lives, robbing us of right relationship with God and one another. In *Little Sins Mean a Lot*, gifted writer Elizabeth Scalia pulls no punches in honestly leading us in a greatly needed collective examination of conscience. But the good news is that this book is not only a look at those sins over which we feel powerless. It's also a friendly companion on the path to total reconciliation, offering teachings of the Church, wisdom from saints and Scripture, and Elizabeth's own companionship along a path to virtue and total healing. An honest, challenging reminder that our souls are worth saving and that sins large and small matter, but that with faith in Christ, hope abounds!"

— Lisa M. Hendey, founder of CatholicMom.com and author of *The Grace of Yes*

"Part examination of conscience, part memoir, part comedy, part poetry, studded with literary and scriptural references, rooted in theology, rounded off with solid, no-nonsense practical advice with real insight into the human psyche, this book is an eye-opener. Funny, wise, easy to read, hard to put down."

— Simcha Fisher, author of *The Sinner's Guide to Natural Family Planning*

"You know that tendency we all have to rationalize bad behavior because it's 'not that big of a deal'? *Little Sins Mean a Lot* will stop that in its tracks — yet leave you feeling energized and hopeful, as if you've just had a fun coffee date with a good friend."

— Jennifer Fulwiler, author of *Something Other Than God*

"We can convince ourselves that we 'are just fine' in our spiritual lives, but Elizabeth Scalia believes that 'little sins' or bad habits are our own worst enemies and a certain gateway to the deadly sins. This one-of-a-kind book piqued my interest in the introduction and had me laughing out loud reading the very first paragraph of chapter 1! Throughout *Little Sins Mean a Lot*, the author cleverly identifies 13 'little sins' using intriguing and witty stories. Very practical solutions are offered, utilizing Scripture, the saints, the *Catechism*, and prayer. A must read!"

— Donna-Marie Cooper O'Boyle, EWTN TV host and award-winning author of 20 books, including *The Kiss of Jesus* (www.donnacooperoboyle.com)

"Elizabeth Scalia has a way of writing that scares me, yet helps me see that I'm not alone. Her writing is like a flashlight that shines light on sins hidden in the dark corners of my soul like dust bunnies under a bed. She doesn't do it in a holier-than-thou way, but rather in a way that says, 'I know, and I'm walking with you,' which is what compassion is all about. This book is a treasure, just like its author."

— Leticia Ochoa Adams, radio host at Breadbox Media and blogger at www.letiadams.com

Little Sins Mean a Lot

Kicking Our Bad Habits Before They Kick Us

Elizabeth Scalia

Our Sunday Visitor

www.osv.com
Our Sunday Visitor Publishing Division
Our Sunday Visitor, Inc.
Huntington, Indiana 46750

Every reasonable effort has been made to determine copyright holders of excerpted materials and to secure permissions as needed. If any copyrighted materials have been inadvertently used in this work without proper credit being given in one form or another, please notify Our Sunday Visitor in writing so that future printings of this work may be corrected accordingly.

Our Sunday Visitor Publishing Division, Our Sunday Visitor, Inc., 200 Noll Plaza, Huntington, IN 46750; 1-800-348-2440

ISBN: 978-1-61278-904-0 (Inventory No. T1690)
eISBN: 978-1-61278-905-7
LCCN: 2016932022

Cover design: Lindsey Riesen
Cover art: Shutterstock
Interior design: Dianne Nelson

PRINTED IN THE UNITED STATES OF AMERICA

For Jamie, Carol, and Jack

Mother-Wounded All
Standing gold amid the dross
Bright chests of wonder

Don't let your sins turn into bad habits.

— St. Teresa of Ávila

—

Don't let your bad habits turn into sins.

— Elizabeth Scalia

Contents

ACKNOWLEDGMENTS

Scripture quotations are from the following versions:

- *Revised Standard Version of the Bible — Second Catholic Edition (Ignatius Edition)* (RSV), copyright © 2006 National Council of the Churches of Christ in the United States of America. Used by permission. All rights reserved.
- *New Revised Standard Version Bible: Catholic Edition* (NRSV), copyright © 1989, 1993 National Council of the Churches of Christ in the United States of America. Used by permission. All rights reserved.
- *New American Bible, revised edition* (NAB), copyright © 2010, 1991, 1986, 1970 Confraternity of Christian Doctrine, Washington, D.C. Used by permission of the copyright owner. All rights reserved. No part of the *New American Bible* may be reproduced in any form without permission in writing from the copyright owner.
- Psalm texts (except Psalms 117 and 119) are from *The Psalms: A New Translation*, copyright © 1963 The Grail (England).
- Psalm 119 is from *The Holy Bible, English Standard Version* (ESV), copyright © 2001 by Crossway, a publishing ministry of Good News Publishers. Used by permission. All rights reserved.

Excerpts from the English translation of *The Roman Missal*, copyright © 2010 International Commission on English in the Liturgy Corporation (ICEL). Excerpts from the English translation of *Liturgy of the Hours*, copyright © 1973, 1974, 1975, ICEL. All rights reserved.

Unless otherwise noted, quotations from papal and other Vatican-generated documents available on vatican.va are copyright © Libreria Editrice Vaticana.

INTRODUCTION

When Bert Ghezzi approached me about writing this book, I gave him a bemused look and said, "You've got to be kidding me. I am a walking, breathing billboard for bad habits, and a cautionary tale against little sins, unattended and left to run rampant."

"Perhaps that is why you should be the one to write it," came the response.

I knew that he was right. Who better to identify and enumerate the small and varied ways in which we sabotage our lives — body, mind, and spirit — than someone who is so self-evidently wallowing in them like a baby elephant in a mud puddle?

The book was meant for me to write because I am intimately aware of the fact that while the big sins we commit in our brokenness can often, and dramatically, impact not only our lives but the lives of others, it's the "little sins" that leave us so mired and weighed down with self-recrimination that our ambitions and our best instincts become thwarted by our own disgust with ourselves. We don't wait for anyone else to make a big "L" out of their thumb and forefinger and smack it to their foreheads to tell us we are "Losers." We can internalize it all by ourselves, because when we are ensnared by the little sins we end up, on some level, hating ourselves. And that affects everything we do, and everyone around us, all the time.

Well, good luck trying to love your neighbor as yourself when you are really sick and tired of *you*. At best, and with God's grace, you can manage to do something good despite yourself, but more often than not, the loving thing you try to do for someone else will end up enmeshed within your familiar web of little sins:

- Perhaps you'll feel so good about what you've done that you'll decide you should reward yourself in the worst way possible, by indulging "just a little" in behavior you know you should not do.
- Perhaps your ego will expect everlasting gratitude and loyalty from the person you have ostensibly "served."
- Perhaps you will decide you could have done better, and bring out the implements of your daily self-flagellation.
- Perhaps, because you have done a good turn for someone, you will feel entitled to talk about them to others.

Ew. Yes, little sins make me hate myself, and not in the good way the saints and the teaching nuns of my youth meant, when they talked about "hating the self for love of Christ and love of others," but in the bad way that makes me feel useless and unlovable and in need of a whole-life makeover. When I feel like that, it is more difficult to go to prayer, more difficult to believe in a God of infinite mercy who is longing for me to long for him.

I mean, what kind of God would want to hang out with a Big-L "loser" like me?

The daily grind of our little sins first wears us down, then wears us out, and too often our faith is lost in the process.

The sins we think of as "big" — like murder, theft, and violence — are often sins of a moment or an impulse; if we are mostly sane, we can admit to them and regret them, and our desire never to repeat them can be a rational and obtainable resolution. After all, we will not go to confession each month and admit to killing someone, or beating on someone, which would not be what anyone would consider a "common" sort of confession. But the "littler" sins of being angry enough to bellow at another in intemperate rage, or to imagine taking a wrench and wailing on them (forgive me, I drive in New York, and these thoughts take hold . . .) are things you might bring up in the confessional month after month. For years.

It's just a common little sin, yes? We've even chuckled about it in the confessional, my priest and I: "Bless me, Father, for I have sinned. I am guilty of being Irish at other people." But as much as we may wave it off and say, "That's just how I am," the "little sin" of daily anger or impatience is a component of wrath, and Christ Jesus warned us about that:

> "You have heard that it was said to your ancestors, 'You shall not kill; and whoever kills will be liable to judgment.' But I say to you, whoever is angry with his brother will be liable to judgment, and whoever says to his brother, 'Raqa,' will be answerable to the Sanhedrin, and whoever says, 'You fool,' will be liable to fiery Gehenna." (Mt 5:21-22, NAB)

"You fool" is pretty mild. "Raqa" is a little tougher; it says to someone, "You're useless." Neither of those expressions are as bad as what I can mutter under my breath at people as I drive on the Long Island Expressway, committing murder in my heart, mile by mile, and almost never remembering to confess it, because "that's just how I am" — as though living with a pilot-light of rage, easily flared and ready for mass slaughter within one's heart, is a normal or healthy thing.

In fact, it is neither normal nor healthy; it is only common — a common little "gateway sin" that connects directly to a deadly one, and is differentiated only by a single word: "intention."

Intention, of course, is what distinguishes a crime punishable-for-life from one that can get you back home. If I run you over with my car, my actual "intention" would determine how a district attorney would charge me. "Did I mean to hit him with my car? No, I was being inattentive and reckless, and I regret that" is one answer, and it would likely get me prison-with-parole, but "Yes, I wanted to run him over; the sonofabitch was wearing a

Red Sox jacket!" will get me a life sentence. In a court of law, one's intention, either way, can seal your fate for the rest of your life. And that's efficient.

Our everyday lives of faith are efficient too. In the first scenario, even with repentance and confession, I might experience a bit of temporal cleansing in purgatory for my unintentional slaughter; but in the second, without repentance, I am going to hell: for me, that probably means an eternity at Fenway Park, with Big Papi always on deck.

Either outcome would have begun with my indulgence of an unintentional "little sin" that inclined me toward the dreadful sin of wrath. I have developed a very bad habit.

The *habit* of sin is what is formed by permitting these "little sins," and the reason they "mean a lot" is because once they become ingrained within us, they shape who we are: mentally, spiritually, and even physically. My size, for instance, is my sin. A too thin or too large person can sometimes fault chemistry for their size (or for at least a part of it), but all too often a fatty like me is hauling around the evidence of gluttony — a "little sin" of a habitually self-indulgent, or self-medicating, bent that might otherwise manifest as alcoholism, were I fond of being drunk, or as a pill-addiction, were I inclined toward benumbed loopiness.

Absent a naturally fast metabolism, a hipless and sinewy female's shape might similarly (though less obviously) be evidence of a gluttony that is as fully fixated on food as I am, coupled with the sin of pride. Someone who watches every morsel he consumes and works out "religiously" might be a paragon of discipline in one respect, but he might also be sacrificing to the idol of the body, through the sin of self-pride.

Wait a second! We've just run through three "little sins" — impatient anger, over-indulgences, and a mania for looking great, and within them we've casually named three of the seven deadly sins: wrath, gluttony, and pride. Am I saying that these smallish faults are actually deadly?

Well, yes. All of our little sins are components — or by-products, if you like — of the capital ones. That's *why* they mean a lot, even if you are "basically a good person."

I mean, I'm basically a good person, and I'm sure you are too, *basically*. What does that actually mean, though?

I'll never forget the first time I heard the phrase, "That doesn't make me a bad person!" A friend had invited a group of us together for supper and had so mangled a not-difficult recipe that we ended up sending out for pizza. He owned up to his error and joked, "But that doesn't make me a bad person."

I laughed at the time but later found myself thinking over those words quite a lot. No, destroying dinner does not make one a bad person, but we say that about ourselves all the time; we've become comfortable with the phrase as a means of self-absolution. "Yeah, okay, I wanted to go medieval on the old lady who never used her blinker and then almost came to a full stop before making a right turn, but that doesn't make me a bad person."

Well, relative to what? Or to whom? Since the sexual and social revolutions, our Judeo-Christian notions of morality — of good and bad, and right and wrong — have been absorbing a broth of rationalism, and the resultant mush we've been eating for nearly 40 years has us regularly burping out, "But I'm a nice/good person," a phrase suggesting that as long as we are not robbing banks, beating our children, blowing up bridges, or kicking puppies, we are doing all right and ought not be held accountable for much, and certainly not judged — even by ourselves — because we're "good."

The thing is, you and I might only be *sort of* good. We don't beat the children and kick the dog. We don't blow up bridges. We don't take what is not ours or plan elaborate schemes for murder. Most of us are meeting minimum standards of good citizenship (which is not the same as good personhood), and we're cognizant enough of those standards to soften the blow when we know we've done wrong:

- "Yeah, I got wasted and hooked up with someone last night, but I'm basically a good person."
- "Yeah, I lied to get out of doing that thing, so he was stuck doing it alone, but that doesn't mean I'm a bad person."
- "Yeah, maybe I could afford to be more generous to my family, or to my church, than I am, but as long as I'm a good person...."

Thus do we convince ourselves, and each other, that we are "fine."

Except that we're not "fine" — we will eventually be judged, and if we are honest with ourselves we know that by clinging to our claim of "basic" goodness, we are damning ourselves with the faintest of praise, and relying on very adolescent, insufficiently formed consciences to guide us.

That doesn't mean we don't want to be good. Obviously we do, which is why we say it, and say it. But what does "goodness" mean?

Those of us who believe we are created by a loving God know that, yes, we are "good." God's creation is permeated with goodness, and some of our Christian mystics, like St. Thérèse Couderc and Thomas Merton, have been permitted to see the light of goodness that suffuses all things. Beyond that innate goodness, though, for which we can take no credit, what exactly entitles us to say, "But I'm a good person ..."?

Am I, really? Are you? I'm inclined to say, "No, not really," and as a witness I will call upon Jesus of Nazareth, who once said, "Why do you call me good? No one is good but God alone" (Mk 10:18, RSV).

If we were naturally good, we would not have needed God to go to the trouble of spelling out to Moses that, no, we can't just abandon our parents when they get old and feeble; we can't just take what we want; we can't kill whom we please and have indiscriminate sex all day long. As obvious as those prohibitions sound to us now, we needed to be told not to do those things — because otherwise we would.

So, we're not "basically good," but Jesus tells us how we can become good, and it boils down to two things: Love God with your whole heart and spirit, and then love the person who is before you at any given moment. The first is seed for the second; if you're really doing the first, the second comes naturally. It is the foundation upon which our authentic goodness is built.

But if we are going to try to become truly good persons, we need to identify and then detach from the faults and sins that we so readily give into, and thus keep us always playing defense.

What we're going to do in this book is identify 13 "little sins" — twelve would have been more biblical, but I couldn't stop myself — that are surprisingly more important to our spiritual and material well-being, and more detrimental to our "basic goodness" than we realize. We will name the sin, flesh it out with the reality of our own experiences, and then take a look at what Scripture, the saints, and (sometimes) the *Catechism of the Catholic Church* have to say about it. Finally, to close each chapter, we will look for some practical solutions — ways and means by which we can begin to break out of the small habitual sins that keep us stuck defending our minimal goodness. And then we'll pray together toward that end.

When I voiced my first objection to taking on this book, it was because I immediately recognized that no one needed it more than I. I anticipate a terrifying bit of self-discovery for me, as I write it. Hopefully, it won't be quite so scary for you to read.

As we begin this journey, though, in your charity, please offer up a small prayer for me.

— Elizabeth Scalia
Feast of the Annunciation, 2015

CHAPTER ONE

Procrastination

Never put off till tomorrow what may be done
day after tomorrow just as well.
— Mark Twain

I am such a champion procrastinator that this book was pitched to me about two years ago. It took me a year to sign the contract. Did you notice the date at the end of my introduction? As I write this, I am contractually bound to deliver this manuscript in about four weeks, and yes, I only just started it this morning.

It's all outlined and in my head, you see, but typing it out is such a drag.

If you were a nice person, wanting to encourage me and validate my life choices, you might respond, "So, you're a procrastinator. So what? We're all a little like that! It doesn't make you a bad person! It's not as if you're hurting anyone!"

Well, I'm not so sure about that. The editor who suggested I write it has been forced to go into editorial meetings where he undoubtedly endured the repeated inquiry, "And how is that Scalia book coming?" I imagine him raising his hands to heaven and saying, "I don't know what her problem is, but she seems like a good person and people tell me she'll deliver. But no, I haven't heard from her."

Already my "little" sin of putting something off has made life difficult for someone other than myself. Editors are waiting; schedulers and designers are waiting. My bank account is waiting.

I can hear you thinking, "But this is not a sin; it's just an inconvenience. It's *maybe* thoughtless, but you're not, like . . . evil."

Thank you for saying I'm not evil. There is no "maybe" about my thoughtless inconveniencing of others, though, and yes, my procrastination is in fact a "little sin" because it is a by-product of a bigger sin, and a deadly one: *sloth*, which the poet Horace called a "wicked siren."

Procrastination is a refusal to engage in the world that is before you. It is an RSVP of "no" to the big and small invitations life is continually offering us. It is also a show of ingratitude toward the gifts and talents that are the source of so many of those (actually flattering) invitations:

- "You want me to write a book? Oh, okay, I'll sign the contract, but really, blogging is so much faster and less structured, so I'll do that for a year, until I really have to think about the deadline."
- "Yes, of course I am still bringing that dessert you love to your dinner, tonight. I just have to go shopping for those ingredients that aren't always easy to find, and it needs six hours to set so . . . I'll try to get to that *this afternoon*."
- "You want me to volunteer to work with the scouts because you're shorthanded and you see that my kids are fairly well functioning? It just means two hours a week and maybe a little prep? Can I get back to you on that? How about next September?"

The life we are given — the only one that you or I will get — is ordered and sustained on the Almighty Affirmation of the Creator. The ever-expanding universe exists and grows through the force of one all-encompassing and wholly intentional idea of YES. "Let there be life" and then *bang!* — or a more slowly evolving *baaaang!* Everything came to be, including you and me.

By your very creation, you and the giftedness that has been bestowed upon you (because we all get at least one gift) have been invited to be a part of the ongoing world: to engage, to grow, to create, to explore; to take everything that comes your way — the good, the less-good, even the mundane — then filter it through your strengths, and share what you've gleaned from it all, with the people around you.

The procrastinator looks at the daily invitation to engage and says, "Mmnnyeah, no" or "I have a thing; now's not a good time" or "Monday. I'll start that on Monday."

"Your first words were not 'Mama' and 'Dada,' " my husband has said to me. "Your parents wanted to believe you were addressing them, but you were actually saying '*Mañana*, baby,' because with you it's always '*mañana*.' "

He might be right. *Mañana* is just a way of saying no until circumstances absolutely force you to say yes. And that's a tepid sort of response to an invitation from God, isn't it? It might even be called "cold."

Is it a sin to say no to God? I'm writing this on the feast of the Annunciation — a day commemorating the visit of the archangel Gabriel, who appeared to the young virgin, Mary, and told her that God's plan for her, were she amenable, was to put her at risk to doubt, ridicule, possible death-by-stoning, and a lifetime of things she would never fully understand:

> In the sixth month, the angel Gabriel was sent from God to a town of Galilee called Nazareth, to a virgin betrothed to a man named Joseph, of the house of David, and the virgin's name was Mary. And coming to her, he said, "Hail, favored one! The Lord is with you." But she was greatly troubled at what was said and pondered what sort of greeting this might be. Then the angel said to her, "Do not be afraid, Mary, for you have found favor with God. Behold, you will conceive in your womb and bear a

son, and you shall name him Jesus. He will be great and will be called Son of the Most High, and the Lord God will give him the throne of David his father, and he will rule over the house of Jacob forever, and of his kingdom there will be no end." But Mary said to the angel, "How can this be, since I have no relations with a man?" And the angel said to her in reply, "The holy Spirit will come upon you, and the power of the Most High will over-shadow you. Therefore the child to be born will be called holy, the Son of God. . . ." Mary said, "Behold, I am the handmaid of the Lord. May it be done to me according to your word." Then the angel departed from her. (Lk 1:26-35, 38, NAB)

The Annunciation is the feast of Mary's great *fiat*, her whole-hearted yes, which put into earthly motion the entire pageant of our salvation. I've often wondered, what if she had said no? What if Mary had listened to Gabriel's words and said, "Say, *whuuut*? You're telling me I'm going to be unwed, and pregnant, and have a crazy-weird life? You can get yourself another girl!"

We know that Mary was gifted with an abundance of graces. Trained in faithfulness, those gifts very likely left her entirely dis-posed to place herself at the service of whatever God, through his messenger, would propose. Her response was a choice, yes, but one that the intensity and richness of her gifted graces might not have permitted her to reject under any circumstances. ("She believed by faith," wrote St. Augustine, and "she conceived by faith.")

Still, though, for the sake of argument, suppose she had said no. Would it have been a sin?

My *instinctive* answer would be no. Beyond the gift of our life itself — the one gift so sacred that it is not ours to refuse or end — God's gifts are freely given and ours to use, misuse, or altogether ignore. Had Mary said no, God *could* have gifted another.

Then again, God had a plan for Mary, and her gifted graces were meant to help her conform to the plan. All she had to do was access what she had been given, and use it.

Which she did. Mary's yes was immediate. She didn't hem-and-haw. She didn't suggest Gabriel come back at a better time. She didn't say, "Let me think about this for a year. . . ." She didn't look for a means of supernatural contraception to ensure that nothing happened until she was good-and-ready for it, if ever.

Mary said yes, and then she immediately engaged, heading off to visit her cousin Elizabeth and pronouncing her Magnificat with perfect trust in God's plan.

I think procrastination is a manifestation of fear that betrays our lack of trust. We believe God has plans for us but still put off doing what it takes to allow the plan to unfold, because we cannot perfectly control the outcome, or control how others will respond to our efforts, or even how we will respond to our own success or failure.

Quintilian said, "We excuse our sloth under the pretext of difficulty." Yes, it is easier to say, "This is hard to do," than to bruise our pride by admitting, "I am afraid."

Because that is true, we stew in our little sin of procrastination. We wait for circumstances to force us out of this cousin to sloth, and then, finally, thrust into projects we have been reluctant to take on, we begin to make our efforts.

And what happens, once we begin? Nine times out of ten, we find ourselves enjoying the thing we've finally gotten around to doing, and that's precisely because we are engaging with our own giftedness, and in a very real way, that is a cooperative engagement with God. We discover, not for the first time, that the thing we'd been putting off was not anywhere near as difficult as we thought it would be. In fact, the most difficult part was simply beginning. Once started, the undertaking we had been dreading became a source of fulfillment.

St. Augustine, who famously asked the Lord to make him chaste, "but *not yet*," would agree, I think. It was when he finally began to embrace his long-delayed chastity that his faith, and subsequently his theological thinking, flowered into its fullness.

I have found this to be true all of my life: whether it involved schooling, a dental appointment, or a big writing project, the hardest part of my undertaking was always just settling down to actually doing the thing I had been putting off — and in the end, the job was usually a snap. I feared I was terrible at science and could never pass an anatomy and physiology class, until I actually took the course and found myself so fascinated that studying and pulling off an A turned out to be a delight and a breeze. I put off having a cracked tooth filling replaced because when I'd gotten it 30 years earlier, dentistry was a lot less pleasant than it is today. When I finally kept my appointment, the thing was done painlessly, in two shakes, and I remembered why I liked my chatty dentist too.

Oh, yeah, and writing. Writers are the biggest procrastinators in the world, because that blank page before us holds a world of possibilities within all of that co-creative engagement — and who can guess where that opening line will lead? The great unknown is terrifying. You can tell how much work a writer has to do by how much time he or she is spending doing other things. My house, for instance, is never cleaner than just before I absolutely, positively must begin to write for a deadline.

When we procrastinate, we make excuses about why so many other things need to be done before we can do the thing we're called to do — the thing we are probably made to do. How often have you heard someone say, "Sure, I want to have kids, right after I do this other thing?" It is just so much easier to go do something (or nothing) else, rather than face our fear with Mary's perfect trust and say, "Behold, I am the hand-servant of the Lord," and then get cracking.

—

WHAT DOES CATHOLICISM SAY
ABOUT PROCRASTINATION?

One can sin against God's love in various ways: . . .

— *acedia* or spiritual sloth goes so far as to refuse the joy that comes from God and to be repelled by divine goodness.
— CATECHISM OF THE CATHOLIC CHURCH (N. 2094)

Let the idleness of vain imaginations be put to flight, let go of sloth, hold fast to diligence. Be instant in holy meditations, cleave to the good things which are of God: leaving that which is temporal, give heed to that which is eternal . . . the sweet contemplations of thy Creator's immeasurable benefits toward thee.
— ST. ANSELM OF CANTERBURY

God has promised forgiveness to your repentance, but He has not promised tomorrow to your procrastination.
— ST. AUGUSTINE

The appetite of the sluggard craves but has nothing, but the appetite of the diligent is amply satisfied.
— PROVERBS 13:4 (NAB)

—

HOW DO WE BREAK THE PATTERN,
OR HABIT, OF PROCRASTINATION?

BEGIN: I don't know whether I heard it from one of my forthright Irish aunties or from a film version of Agatha Christie's hardy Miss Marple, but in my memory resides the voice of an older woman pronouncing six words that always made great sense to me: "Begin as you mean to continue!" It's good advice that orders us to do the hardest part first: Begin! Just walk up to the thing you know you want to do, but are dawdling about, and get started. Once you connect with the divine spark within you — that giftedness that inspired the project idea to start with — the chances are you will discover that you're enjoying yourself, that you're glad you've begun, and that the thing really isn't terribly difficult at all. How sad that it has taken me the better part of my life to realize this.

DO NOT BE AFRAID: Now that we've established that there is an element of fear connected to our procrastination, we can acknowledge it, identify what precisely it is that we are afraid of, and then push through that fear, confident in the knowledge that whenever we consent to a co-creative engagement with God and the gifts he has bestowed upon us — whether we do it immediately, like Mary, or after some reluctant dawdling, like Augustine — we can trust God with the outcome. We know that our acquiescent engagement with what is before us will not leave us deprived of anything but, rather, enriched in surprising ways because that is how God works. As Teresa of Ávila said, "God withholds himself from no one who perseveres."

HAND YOUR HESITANCY OFF TO HEAVEN: St. Benedict of Nursia recommended to his monks that before undertaking anything — be it cooking, studying, or even a leisurely walk — they first offer a short prayer, asking God's blessings upon the focus of their energies. We don't do this enough, and that is particularly sad when you consider that we have heaven and its occupants at our disposal. Our guardian angels are always with us, and if we ask for their assistance it is always given; the saints in heaven are assigned patronages to assure that we are never left without spiritual guidance and intercessory prayers, no matter what the task. So, if you are putting off going to confession, St. John Vianney's companionship is yours for the claiming. When my husband put off a woodworking project for several years, I gave up asking. Consigning him to the intercession of St. Joseph was effective in finally getting things started. As I have buckled down to write this book, my icon of St. Francis de Sales, patron of writers and journalists, has been ever before me, and I only wish that the tale of St. Expeditus were true. In Latin America, Expeditus is usually depicted holding aloft a cross, inscribed with the word *hodie* (Latin, "today"), while simultaneously stomping on a crow (or, sometimes, a snake) labeled *cras* (Latin, "tomorrow"). In Germany, he points at a clock, reminding us not to waste time. No "*Mañana*, baby" for him!

Regrettably, the hagiography of Expeditus is one of those delightful bits of bungling that occur within a 2,000-year history of a worldwide church. According to John Delaney's *Dictionary of Saints*, Expeditus may have been created by some nuns whose Latin was a bit shaky.

> **St. Expeditus (no date), Patron saint of UPS, FEDEX, DHL, and USPS?**
> "Mentioned in the Roman Martyrology as one of a group of martyrs who were executed in Militene, Armenia, there is no proof he ever existed. The popular devotion to him may have mistakenly developed when a crate of holy relics from the Catacombs in Rome to a convent in Paris was mistakenly identified by the recipients as St. Expeditus by the word *expedito* written on the crate. They began to propagate devotion to the imagined saint as the saint to be invoked to expedite matters, and the cult soon spread. [Feast day,] April 19" (*Dictionary of Saints*, by John Delaney).

I confess, I love the idea of a St. Expeditus, dedicated to helping us deal with the little sin of putting things off — but, lacking him, perhaps St. Augustine will do, coupled with St. Jude Thaddeus, the patron of desperate causes.

Pray
(THIS PRAYER OR YOUR OWN)

Lord, you created the universe on the strength of your own intention, and sustain the world throughout space and time, which, for you, are neither linear nor limited. Please look upon me, your sometimes time-and-space-challenged child, with patience. Help me to overcome the fears and bad habits that so often prevent me from setting to the tasks you have placed before me, that I might know and serve you better. All good things come from you, and the requests for my help, for my assistance, and for my participation in the world and among my neighbors are good things I need to better appreciate. In your mercy, give me the strength, the energy, the firmness of resolve, and the trust I need so that I might move forward into my work, at the center of which I will discover the depths of your mysterious love for me. I ask this, as ever, in the name of your Son, Christ Jesus. Amen.

—

St. Augustine and St. Jude Thaddeus, unofficial
patrons of slacking-off procrastinators,
Ora pro nobis; ora pro me!

CHAPTER TWO

Excessive Self-Interest

But enough about me, let's talk about you.
What do you think of my children? Aren't they cute?
— One of your friends (or, uh, you?)

Have you ever shared something of yourself with someone else — something meaningful and life-affecting — and had the person you're talking to say, "Oh, that happened to me," and who then proceeded to turn the conversation to herself?

It's certainly happened to me, and more than once. I'm sure it has happened to you. Every young couple excitedly anticipating their wedding or the birth of a child has had the experience of announcing their happy news (or sharing their anxieties) only to be regaled with stories from well-meaning people who can't wait to share their own experiences, and they're usually cautionary tales ("Let me tell you about Italian mothers-in-law; your meatballs will never be right!") or outright horror stories ("Thirty-six hours I was in labor, and I didn't just have front labor, I had back labor; I had thigh labor; I never screamed so much!").

Over the years, it has seemed to me there might be some element of mischief to all of these stories — I am positive that one of my aunties took secret delight in turning my husband pale with her stories of projectile vomiting, overflowing diapers with neon-colored offerings, and well-intentioned nursing adventures gone horribly awry.

For the most part, though, when people share such stories, they're not trying to steal anyone's thunder or stick a wedge into someone's happiness. In an odd way, they're trying to share in it.

When our son became engaged, and we related some of our experiences in dealing with the traditions and expectations of others, we quite naturally fell into retelling our own horror stories. We weren't indifferent to our son or his bride, but we could only speak to what we knew, and that necessarily meant turning the subject us-ward. In situations such as these, people end up talking about themselves, often at length, because it's what they know. In a way, they are helpfully demonstrating that the difficult things bridal couples and new parents focus on so intently become — with hindsight and the balm of time — hilarious memories.

Such oversharing is usually well intended, and most of the time it does not leave us feeling like we have just played straight man for the gratuitous amusement of an empathy-challenged narcissist who is, in the end, quite indifferent to us.

The "little sin" of excessive self-interest is distinct from narcissism, which is a personality disorder and a legitimate illness, because it involves us making a choice to prefer our own interests, our own stories, and our own voices over those around us.

Not long ago I had lunch with a few business associates, men I had corresponded with but never met. After discussing work issues, which I managed to do like an adult human being, we quite naturally began to chat about our families and personal lives, and that's where my circuitry went a little haywire. Both gentlemen managed to mention their spouses and children with obvious pride and affection, but with what I would call a seemly restraint.

Not so, Lizzie. Oh ... not so.

Now, I grant you, I work from home and sometimes will go a whole day without the opportunity to use my tongue, so when I get around people I can be a bit of a motormouth, and I know it. On this particular afternoon, I had been housebound due to illness; it had literally been weeks since I'd had real conversations with anyone beyond my family, so the pump was primed. Once I began talking about my sons, I lost all sense of professional decorum and began to gush like a broken water main.

The men were perfectly tolerant of the torrent, but while my mouth was flapping, my guardian angel began shouting an interior cue that sounded a lot like begging, or a heavenly face palm: "Please . . . *stop* . . . *talking.* Ask *them* something about *their* kids, like a normal person would!"

Finally, I was thrown a six-word lifesaver: "You mentioned your son studies biology," I said to the man on my left, and as he answered I felt myself mercifully pulled out from the verbal deluge, only slightly worse for wear.

The devilish spirit of excess thus departed from me, but only because I really wanted it to, and had made a choice to let someone else brag a little, and to actually be present to, and enjoy, the pride he took in his son. I could just as easily have chosen to ignore my better angel and prattled on until my companions, lacking guns, or ropes from which to hang themselves, instead scalded their throats with hot coffee swallowed too fast, in order to end the meal and make their escape.

Excessive self-interest involves choosing to either be considerate of others or completely immune to them. It is a "little sin" for certain, because when we indulge it, we tend to stop seeing the equally interesting humanity of the people around us. They become utilitarian objects; receptacles for our endless streams of me-thought and mine-words. We overwhelm them with our yelps or burden them with our yokes; and although it might — at first consideration — seem like a measure of insecurity is involved in this excess ("*Seems*, madam? Nay, it is!"), all of it, even the insecurity, is a function and by-product of pride.

I have a friend who is a terrific conversationalist. He can chat extensively with anyone, and do it with a good deal of empathy and charm. People love to talk with him because he manages to convey the sort of warm and lively interest that makes people feel good about themselves. He chooses to be friendly to people who are friendly to him, with one exception. That exception is me. No matter how I try to fall into the "friendly chat" category, I never quite make it. In the odd moment when I manage to squeeze in a few words, he will look away and keep talking — about anything at all that is going on in his life — as long as it means not engaging with anything at all that is going on in mine.

It wasn't always that way, but over the past 20 years or so he has become unsure of himself around me, and therefore afraid, and in that state of insecurity his choice is to protect himself with a wall of words. At a picnic a few years ago, I deliberately brought up issues in my life, just to see if I could raise any sort of authentic response from him, toward the actuality of my presence and my personhood. As expected, I could not. Any subject I tried to broach he immediately used to completely ignore me by turning the subject to himself. If I mentioned a child's recent bout of bronchitis, he spoke to the air about nearly dying of pneumonia; when I mentioned a sudden opportunity to visit Vienna, he had a long cruise to think and talk about.

It was a little like playing tennis with someone and having every serve volleyed back, over the head, with no possibility of engagement.

Eventually, I gave him the serve; I stopped talking about myself — thus offering him no chance to lob a topic out of reach — and instead just flat out asked, "So, what's new with you?"

He simply said, "Nothing."

Nothing. Game incomplete. There was absolutely no way he was going to directly respond to, or acknowledge, anything about my life, and he certainly wasn't going to give me any sort of opening by answering, as he might to another, "Nothing, what's new with you?" I understood — probably better than he did — that he had made a choice to block me, until I was effectively absent from his presence.

Another friend had watched the whole exchange and said to me, later, "Wow, he really hates you."

"No," I disagreed. "I think he actually loves me a lot, which is why he can't bear to be around me."

"That makes no sense," he said.

"It does. Once I told him something I thought he needed to know; it turns out he didn't. He thought I was trying to be cruel. Now, he can only feel bad around me, so he does that thing you saw."

He looked at me askance: "Were you cruel? Intentionally?"

"No, I really wasn't, not intentionally," I said, sadly. "I was just very, very stupid, and stupidity made me cruel."

That, of course, was my own prideful mistake, and guess what? It was born of excessive self-interest. The self-help movement of the 1990s, which I had bought into, taught me to focus excessively upon myself, and to "honor myself" — like a little idol — by burdening another with an offering of truth best left unshared. Everything that followed came from my own terribly grave and destructive little sin of me-ism, taken to an unhealthy extreme.

Here be monsters. In the case of that relationship, as no opening to ask forgiveness will be permitted, what healing may come between us, at this point, I leave to God's discretion, and to the prayers of good friends.

And I impugn no sin on the one unwilling to engage with me. I think his unwillingness may fall under Just War guidelines, as a necessary means of self-preservation. Like the *Catechism* says, "The act of self-defense can have a double effect: the preservation of one's own life; and the killing of the aggressor. . . . The one is intended, the other is not"[1] (n. 2263).

I indict only myself, a witless and self-interested aggressor.

—

WHAT DOES CATHOLICISM SAY ABOUT EXCESSIVE SELF-INTEREST?

"Greater love has no man than this, that a man
lay down his life for his friends."
— John 15:13 (RSV)

If I speak in the tongues of men and of angels, but have not love, I
am only a noisy gong or a clanging cymbal.... Love is ...
not boastful; it is not arrogant.
— 1 Corinthians 13:1, 4-5 (RSV)

Let no one seek his own good, but the good of his neighbor.
— 1 Corinthians 10:24 (RSV)

It is always the secure who are humble.
— G. K. Chesterton

Stay quiet with God. Do not spend your time in useless chatter....
Do not give yourself to others so completely that you
have nothing left for yourself.
— St. Charles Borromeo

The only reason why the Immaculate permits us to fall is
to cure us from our self-conceit, from our pride, to make
us humble and thus make us docile to the divine graces.
— St. Maximilian Kolbe

It was pride that changed angels into devils;
it is humility that makes men as angels.
— St. Augustine

It is better for you to have little than to have much which may
become the source of pride.
— THOMAS À KEMPIS, *THE IMITATION OF CHRIST*

There never can have been, and never can be,
and there never shall be any sin without pride.
— ST. AUGUSTINE

We put pride into everything, like salt.
— ST. JOHN VIANNEY

—

HOW DO WE BREAK AWAY FROM THE SIN, OR HABIT, OF EXCESSIVE SELF-INTEREST?

LISTEN: "Listen" is the first word of the Holy Rule of St. Benedict, and it is the word whose application can speak to a multitude of sins, because if we are listening, we are not talking. If we are listening, we are mindful not of ourselves but of our surroundings. When we are listening, we are hearing and being present to the person who is before us. When we are truly present to others, we find ourselves relieved of the *burden* of ourselves, and often we discover that our own thoughts need adjusting, thanks to what we have heard.

LIMIT TIME ON SOCIAL MEDIA: Nothing so trains us to obsess over ourselves, and how others perceive us, or to stew over our own musings, as social media. Twitter encourages us to think of a brief, under-thought pronouncement delivered w/*unpunctuated wrds like dis* as something so wise and witty that we feel comfortable barging into the conversations of others to share it. Facebook tells us that our every thought is a likable one, our children are, at all times, too adorable for words, and our "friends" think we are absolutely brilliant, for as long as we agree with them. The temptation to remain agreeable, keep your thoughts in the acceptable box, and keep serving up the praise-fodder is enormous and seductive. How can you emerge from spending a few hours, every day, in such an environment and not develop an excessive sense of your imprint on the world, and the wonderfulness that is you?

LEARN TO MAKE A DAILY EXAMEN: The Ignatian practice of a daily examen is an antidote to the superficial uplift we find on social media; it allows us to still focus upon ourselves, but in a more analytical and balanced way. It is brief spiritual exercise devised by St. Ignatius of Loyola that can help you become refocused on what matters, and spiritually refreshed and renewed. Sitting quietly in a comfortable (but not nap-encouraging) position, you work your way through five steps:

1. You bring yourself into awareness of God's presence by thanking him for what you noticed during the day that made you aware of his grace. Perhaps your attention was captured by birdsong, or a beautiful sunrise, and you have a momentary sense of God's grandeur. Perhaps you wondered at your children and realized that they all are precisely the people you met at their birth, personalities already intact, and you saw God's design in their individuality. Whatever touched you, remember it, and express thanks to God.

2. Go over the day, asking God to make you aware of where he had especially been with you.

3. Consider how you felt over the course of the day — where you had lost your temper, or felt left out, or confused, or really joyful. This is also a time to be honest with God, and with yourself, about "what I have done and ... what I have failed to do." As in maybe you really did spend way too much time on Facebook and failed to pay attention to something someone you love was saying to you. Maybe you didn't listen well.

4. Ask forgiveness for your failings and for your sins, little and bigger. If one particular moment stands out, ask God to give you wisdom on that matter so that you might learn from it. Be eager for instruction. We can never go wrong by echoing Solomon's prayer for "an understanding heart."

5. Ask for the graces to do better tomorrow, and let God know that you gratefully look forward to a new day.

An examen is not terribly time-consuming. St. Benedict might have said of the examen that it "contains nothing harsh or burdensome" because it is merely a review of the day between you and God, but it is a review that covers all of the spiritual bases: it begins not with a "please" but with a "thank you," and then manages an apology where needed before asking for anything more. Taking these 10 or 15 minutes a day to meet and talk to God is an amazingly simple yet powerful way to increase our capacity for mindfulness, which will make us better aware of other people.

That will, in short order, lessen the sinful excesses of our own self-interest.

PRAY
(THIS PRAYER OR YOUR OWN)

Heavenly Father, your psalmist begged, "Set, O Lord, a guard over my mouth; / keep watch at the door of my lips!" (Ps 141:3). So often our mouths and our minds are reckless, running by the full force of our egos. We are so interested in being seen, and noticed, and thought well of by others, that we ironically render ourselves unable to see those very same people — and then, by our thoughtlessness, we injure them; we use them as sounding boards or reflecting mirrors, rather than respecting the dignity with which you have endowed their humanity. Please help me to keep a watch on my own excesses, that I may be more eager to see than to be seen; more willing to hear than to be heard — all that your creation may be better served. In Christ's name, I pray. Amen.

CHAPTER THREE

Self-Neglect

Self-love, my liege, is not so vile a sin
As self-neglecting.
— *Henry V*, Act II, Scene IV

Flannery O' Connor once proclaimed that "half of writing is overcoming the revulsion you feel when you sit down to it." As I demonstrated in the chapter on procrastination, she is quite right. Of all the chapters I have desperately tried to avoid writing for this book, I have felt real revulsion at the prospect of pulling this one from my brain because it touches on too many home truths. I've always said self-effacement is a much easier discipline than facing the self.

A couple of years ago, discussing a public figure with a young Catholic writer, I wondered about whether our subject was as narcissistic as it was claimed. He looked down upon me, mostly because I am short, and said, "You could use a little of his narcissism."

When people make spontaneous comments touching on my looks, I never know how to receive it, and therefore I rarely make a response. I'm always too busy trying to figure out whether they were complimenting me or expressing dismay.

That's not a joke. In my youth, I had managed a brief moment of svelte prettiness that always seemed to bring out the lecher in crass sorts of men (and occasionally crass women), and it always left me wary and wondering. Having become plump in my 30s, I recall meeting a woman on the street who exclaimed, and loudly, "What happened to you? You used to weigh 80 pounds!"

Mistaking my silence and dumb look for a rebuke, she telephoned later to apologize, and I had no idea how to explain to her that my silence was not meant as a censure: I'd simply been trying to figure out if I had ever looked as good as she seemed to think. In my own mind, I have always been a hideous specimen, which perhaps explains why it is that, while I love looking at fashion and fabric, and shoes, I think of them as "not for me." I generally wander about wearing years-old black clothing and plastic Crocs on my feet. It occurs to me that, having never felt like much of a gift to anyone, wrapping myself up in pretty colors and topping myself off with a bow would seem a bit like false advertising.

Is that self-loathing? Sure, it is, in spades. If excessive self-love can come from a place of insecurity, self-neglect comes from a place of hate and anger — from a place where God is not, because we do not extend an invitation to God to join us in our interior squalor.

That is to our detriment, though, because if we would only invite him in, he would come. And then, where God is, what has been empty becomes full; what has been dark becomes light; what has been plundered can be made whole. The job is neither easy nor fast, but eventually our interior restoration cannot help, in those circumstances, to eventually become reflected in our exterior.

Pondering that, I scald at my own bad habits and the deficient understanding that has allowed them to take such hardy root within me, for so long, because it has only made my restoration a bigger undertaking than it might have been 20 or 30 years earlier.

Back when my companion recommended that I embrace a measure of narcissism, I was left with questions:

- Why would someone advise me toward narcissism?
- Is my self-neglect so obvious?

- But it's a good and humble thing, is it not, to be unconcerned about the body and how it is clothed and whether or not I am in fashion?

I didn't pursue the answers, at that time, because if I had, they would have been obvious:

- Because look at yourself, woman!
- Yes.
- Umm, well ... you're confusing detachment, which is a good and humble thing, with treating and dressing yourself in a manner wholly distinct from the way you treat or dress the people you actually love.

Oh — and *ow*.

Yeah, that stung to write. And I bet a lot of parents reading that last bit might identify with it, and feel a bit stung too.

Particularly when our children are very young — or our parents are very old — we get into the habit of putting ourselves last in the list of priorities. We take care of the kids, or the parents; take care of the house; take care of the spouse; take care of whatever is coming up on the calendar, and if there is any time left over, take care of ourselves — but, really, we're not that important.

Ah, this sounds so unselfish; it must be holy, right?

I used to think so. Now, I believe there is a point where our selfless actions become paradoxically egotistical and slightly mad.

If, by our appearance, we are wearing a big sign that says, "I put everyone else's needs before mine," we're actually, in a passive way, making ourselves the center of attention. In a sense, we are functioning in a reverse Munchausen-by-proxy sort of world: rather than making our children sick in order to glean some sympathetic concern and attention from others, we're spit-shining our family and friends in hopes of a martyr's accolades: *Such self-sacrifice is so seldom seen!*

Except it never really plays out that way; people noticing a bedraggled, unkempt parent don't think, "Wow, that noble mom is all for her children!" They think, "Oy, those poor kids! Look what's modeling adulthood for them!"

Note the "what" in that sentence. The humanity of a self-neglectful adult is always diminished in society, as people see the bulkiness, the faded clothes, and messy hair and form their judgments long before they see the human being beneath all that. And unfairly or not, those judgments will often get turned toward the children, as well.

I recall, many years ago, a letter someone had written to either Ann Landers or Dear Abby. The writer was a woman who confessed that while she had allowed her children to play with the kids of a neighboring family, she had never extended friendship toward the mother, someone she described as an overweight and untidy "disaster." As the family moved away, the writer received a handwritten note from the disaster, wishing her well and praising her children, who had been good friends to her own young ones. That the note had been "written with a fountain pen, in a beautiful hand, on very tasteful stationery" threw the writer for a loop; she realized that this other mother seemed to share her values, tastes, and habits and might have actually been someone she would have liked, had she not been so put off by a disheveled appearance. She felt guilty for how quickly and superficially she had made up her mind about someone who might have been a fine friend.

The response from Ann or Abby was a variation of "Well, now you know better, so next time don't judge a book by its cover," which is a great sentiment, but we all do judge things by appearances, all the time.

The lesson someone like me needed to take away from that missive was "Take care of yourself, to avoid unfair judgments

against you and yours." Instead, I have always remembered to
practice my penmanship and keep a fountain pen and nice stationery in the house.

So, if someone judges my appearance, I can guilt them with
an elegantly wrought, gilt-edged note, I guess. Egad, that doesn't
sound passive-aggressive at all, does it?

All jokes aside, though, it's much easier to keep good pen and
paper at the ready than to deal with the self, and I seemed to intuit
that at a young age.

The thing is, there is — there has to be — a balanced and
sane place in between the sin of narcissism and the sin of walking
around carrying excessive amounts of extra weight (or a foggy,
alcohol-or-sugar-related hangover), all ungroomed and wearing
rags.

And yeah, it is a sin; hatred of a human person and neglect
of a human body are sins, even if the hate and neglect are "only"
directed toward the self, because they involve complete disrespect
toward God, as he is revealed in his creation. That creation would
be you, yourself. That creation would be me, myself. What God
loves into being, we have no right to mistreat or dishonor.

We recognize the inherent sin of it all when we treat others
this badly — I've certainly logged plenty of time in the confessional admitting to my shameful hatred for another person, or
my sins of omission, when I have not reached out to help another.
Why don't we recognize it when it comes to hating and neglecting
ourselves?

In a way, I suppose, we can blame the saints. We read about
saints giving everything they had to the poor and wearing coarse
or donated clothes, and it all sounds so romantic and detached
from worldly things that we can believe our self-neglect says
something good about our spiritual state.

Perhaps, to an extent, it does. None of us need 50 pairs of
shoes or walk-in closets full of so many outfits that we cannot pos-

sibly wear them all — and it is probably a very good thing if we can keep our lives simple and our possessions few. But those possessions should be presentable, and so should we, both to honor God — to show that we value what God has valued in us — and also that we may be *trusted* to value others.

As he was cataloging some of his own health issues and a recent hospital stay, radio personality Don Imus talked about the nurses he had encountered. Praising them as "wonderful, generous people" and "real angels," he nevertheless wondered why female nurses (not, interestingly enough, the males) were often overweight and sometimes obese. "The nicest ones," he marveled, were often "the meatiest," and "meaty nurses" seemed incongruous amid health professionals.

Imus' cohorts were quick to point out that nurses are some of the hardest working people in the world, who frequently work through their meals or grab a bite of whatever happens to be around — often goodies brought to them by grateful families. Their remarks were fair, but Imus had inadvertently touched on the matter of trust. For some patients, a chubby nurse might feel approachably warm and mom-like, but many others might wonder, "How do I know you'll pay attention to me if you are not really paying attention to you?"

It is the same in the world. People are self-concerned. If they are seeking help or advice, or trying to fill a post (even, perhaps especially, a service-oriented or pastoral one), how do they know they can trust us to be attentive, serious, and capable of identifying and meeting their needs if we seem less-than-attentive, serious, or capable of identifying and meeting our own?

There is an ironic rub to all of this. Speaking only anecdotally, it has been my experience that some of the biggest-hearted, most generous people I've ever known — the ones who go into nursing and mental-health professions and who seek out opportunities to do volunteer work and help others — are people who don't do a great job of taking care of themselves. My instinct is that some people who have been undervalued in their own lives convert the confusion and pain of being neglected into empathic action for others. Love will always out; perhaps for these people, the love and compassion they've learned not to expend on themselves must find expression somewhere, and thus extends outward, toward others.

If so, this becomes part-and-parcel of the great mystery of love and pain that we see in the crucified Christ: only great love can bear great pain, and then convert that pain into even greater love, but not for the self.

And yet, even Christ Jesus, the great self-sacrificing Messiah, did not confuse sacrifice with self-neglect: he asked people for what he needed, whether it was a cup of water, or a solitary retreat from stressful demands, or a room for the Passover Seder. He expected what, culturally, he had coming to him ("You gave me no water for my feet, but she has bathed my feet with her tears and dried them with her hair" [Lk 7:44, NRSV]). As he moved from town to town, preaching and healing, he even managed to acquire a seamless tunic that was nice enough for people to argue over as he was dying.

In other words, Jesus may have sacrificed himself, but he also respected himself. Valuing his own personhood, he did not neglect himself, either through self-loathing or a backward need to demonstrate his humility. In Jesus, there is no sin, so the grave, deadly sins that are connected to our self-hate — and, depending on our individual stories, they can involve some or all combinations of gluttony, sloth, wrath, and even pride — had no way to develop in him.

How does pride fit into self-loathing? Well, Jesus knew who he was: one begotten and beloved of God, and he told us that we, too, are beloved. If we accept the omniscience of God, then how much pride must we possess in order to decide that our understanding is better than God's, and therefore our self-hate and self-neglect is justified?

—

WHAT DOES CATHOLICISM SAY ABOUT SELF-NEGLECT?

God planned in the fullness of time to restore all things in Christ.

— ANTIPHON 3, EVENING PRAYER, WEEK II, LITURGY OF THE HOURS

Praised be the God and Father
of our Lord Jesus Christ,
who has bestowed on us in Christ
every spiritual blessing in the heavens.

God chose us in him
before the world began
to be holy
and blameless in his sight.

He predestined us
to be his adopted sons through Jesus Christ,
such was his will and pleasure,
that all might praise the glorious favor
he has bestowed on us in his beloved.

In him and through his blood, we have been redeemed,
and our sins forgiven,
so immeasurably generous
is God's favor to us.

God has given us the wisdom
to understand fully the mystery,
the plan he was pleased
to decree in Christ.

A plan to be carried out
in Christ, in the fullness of time,
to bring all things into one in him,
in the heavens and on earth.
— EPHESIANS 1:3-10 (LITURGY OF THE HOURS)

There is not a sacrifice sweeter or more agreeable to God than obedience. Obedience is better than sacrifice, says the Scripture.
— ST. IGNATIUS OF LOYOLA

Perfection cannot be attained without the greatest toil.
— ST. PHILIP NERI

[One must] regard all utensils and goods of the [household] as sacred vessels of the altar, aware that nothing is to be neglected.
— RULE OF ST. BENEDICT (CHAPTER 31)

Whoever fails to keep the things belonging to the [household] clean or treats them carelessly should be reproved....
— RULE OF ST. BENEDICT (CHAPTER 32)

—

HOW DO WE BREAK AWAY FROM THE SIN, OR HABIT, OF EXCESSIVE SELF-INTEREST?

GROUND YOUR EXPECTATIONS IN REALITY: Look, if pulling ourselves together was easy, there would be no multibillion-dollar market for self-help books, exercise programs, and "amazing" new diets; there would be no infomercials suggesting that if we just buy the right doodad, or sign on for a particular beauty/fitness regime, or attend the correct motivational seminar, we will be better, more lovable, more acceptable people. Instead, every season brings new titles, new programs, and new ways to spend money on external solutions to what is, at root, the most interior of problems: we're not wholly connected to God; we love him but we don't deliver unto him our whole selves, because — not trusting ourselves to do the right thing — we don't trust God enough, either.

Jesus told us, "In my father's house are many rooms" (Jn 14:2, RSV); so there are within each of us. The rooms we like within ourselves, we open up to God, but those other rooms — the rooms we hate — we keep closed off from him; we neglect them and allow them to fall into ruin. In my own life, I have loved God enough to entertain him in my better rooms, the parts of myself that I judge to be "okay" — but the rest? Slammed shut. All of my hours of prayer, all of my efforts at volunteerism, and all of my earnest personal resolve count as nothing when weighed against the fact that I had not trusted God enough to invite him into the worst of my rooms and asked him — the Master Builder! — for his help with my restoration. Finally doing so has made all the difference, in ways another self-help title never could.

THINK: St. Jerome wrote, "Either we must speak as we dress, or dress as we speak. Why do we profess one thing and display another?" Whatever forms our habits of self-neglect take, if we can do better, then we really must, for the sake of honoring God and his creation, and for honest witness. If I take my dog for a walk and she is unkempt, what people will take away from seeing her is that I am neglectful of this creature I purport to love. When we go out in public looking scattershot and undergroomed, we give no glory to God but instead suggest that he, too, is neglectful of us.

But we know we are not neglected by God, only by ourselves, and our habit of not really *thinking* about how we look. Over a weekend, take a look at the clothes and necessary accessories you have been using: Are they ragged and stained, and better suited for cleaning the garage? When was the last time you got a good haircut? No one in the world actually "needs" a designer handbag, but are you carrying around something that really needs a thorough cleaning or even replacement? A little mindfulness about one's appearance is not vanity; it is verification that you are not ignorant of God's love for you.

TAKE SMALL STEPS OF RESTORATION: If we have the ability to get more exercise, make better choices with our food and drink, read better material, and purchase a respectable pair of shoes and modest-but-presentable clothing, then we owe it to ourselves, to the world, and to God to each day make some effort to pull away from the easy neglect of the self.

We are a royal priesthood. We are daughters and sons of the King. As such, our public tribute to him must involve a daily acknowledgment that our minds and bodies really are the temples within which our own small spirits meet his Holy One. My own temple had grown less-than-presentable, and I allowed that for too long. These days, my daily prayer includes a request for help in recognizing where I need to pull myself together, and also for the fortitude to make at least one small, positive change in how I am getting through my day.

The answers come in surprising ways: one day I felt prompted to put on a little lipstick and a seldom-worn blazer before dropping something off at a friend's house. Those small actions made me feel more put-together, and I realized, as I packed the car, that I was carrying myself a little differently. Maybe it was the blazer, but I felt a touch of unaccustomed sureness about me. When my friend opened the door, she blurted out, "Wow, you look terrific!" — which further buoyed my sense of confidence. Reviewing the scene at the end of the day, in my examen, it was an opportunity to thank God, or his angels, for the prompting, for the pleasant exchange with my friend, for the feeling I had experienced, all throughout the day, of being better-acquainted with a stronger side of myself. I can't say I managed lipstick the next day — my lifelong habit of neglect is still my default-mode, but deliberate mindfulness, a little prayer and a little corresponding action, every day, is slowly but surely creating new, better habits.

Inviting God into my less-tidy rooms and seeking his help for my interior restoration has begun to reflect on my exterior. Given my body type, my endocrine system, my age, and my genetics, I do not expect to ever again be svelte, but things are nevertheless changing for the better. My lifelong battle with my weight continues, but there is more exercise. There are fewer binges, and overall, my health is better. When I do occasionally drop a size, I no longer regain it in two weeks. Everyone's mileage may vary, but this is real restoration, for me, borne of realistic expectations.

I have also come to realize that restoration does not mean erasure. In visiting Dublin, Ireland, one can appreciate the post-revolution growth and renewal of the city, while still noting the bullet holes that give testament to a difficult history. I expect this will be the case for me too, but that is not necessarily a bad thing. The bullet holes and scars of Dublin mar its beauty, but only slightly; they also make it more interesting, because we know there is history there, and therefore lessons to glean from it, if we are inclined to pursue them.

PRAY

(THIS PRAYER OR YOUR OWN)

Well, Lord, here we are. Welcome to my temple, which I have allowed to fall into some disrepair. You've seen the better rooms; please be with me now, as I attempt to show you into my messier ones. These rooms I can barely go into myself, because they have become unpleasing, unattractive, uninhabitable, and full of fug. Will you help me to restore what can be saved, and to discard what cannot? Help me to see these rooms with your eyes, with all their stains and scars, but also with all their potential. And then, if you please, give me the fortitude to — each day — attend to some small repair: a bit of spackle over one small hole, today; a little soldering of a stray wire, tomorrow; the hammering down of a floorboard that keeps tripping me up. In this way, with your help, I know that I will finally be able to recover those rooms I have left to stagnate. I will finally be able to see and reclaim more of the fullness of your gifts to me — and in so doing, I will thankfully be able to make you more welcome into my life. In the name of your Son, Jesus, the Christ, I beg your merciful help in my wholehearted pursuit of my own restoration, to your greater glory. Amen.

CHAPTER FOUR

"Treat Yo'self!":
When Small Indulgences Take Over

Life is short; eat dessert first.
— Attributed to many

A memorable episode of NBC's *Parks and Recreation* involved two of the series' most flamboyant characters, Tom and Donna, inviting the uptight budget-manager Ben along, as they spend a day relaxing and indulging all of their material whims.

"I really want this dress," Donna says, emerging from a dressing room, "and I like this crystal beetle, but it's expensive, and there's no use for it."

"Donna Meagle," replies Tom before a confused Ben, "Treat yo'self!"

Then Tom models his own choices: "Velvet slippies; cashmere socks; velvet pants; cashmere turtle: I'm a cashmere-velvet candy cane!"

To which Donna emphatically replies, "Treat yo'self!"

Ben, who has been observing this behavior in quiet befuddlement, breaks the fourth wall, and says to the viewer, "This is *insane.*"

Part of the joke is that Tom and Donna both know it. They completely understand how absurd and over-the-top they are being with their outlandish self-pampering, which is why they only permit themselves to enjoy it one day a year; any more than that and their harmless lark would morph into something desperate, needy, and sad. It would require rationalizations against common sense, and spiritual health, that neither character would have the interest or energy to come up with.

Most of us aren't looking to spend a cartoonish day buying stuff we don't need, but we all have little ways we "treat" ourselves, and to rationalize it we adopt a Hobbesian spin: life is nasty, brutish, and short, and so we deserve the splurge. Those unfamiliar with Hobbes break it down to YOLO: *You only live once.*

There's nothing morally wrong with an occasional small indulgence, particularly in the midst of something festive — even during Lent: after all, we are permitted to exempt ourselves from our disciplines on Sundays, because a day of Resurrection must be celebrated. For many of us, however, particularly in the prosperous West — and even more particularly, I might say, in the United States — treating ourselves has become an everyday sort of thing. One of my friends recently wondered what she should give her son for his 21st birthday. "He has everything," she lamented, "and this has been the problem since he was 12! I never know what to get him for his birthday or Christmas, because no one waits anymore to get stuff on special occasions. It's not like when we were kids!"

She was right, and we both reminisced about the excitement we felt as children, when the approach of a birthday or Christmas meant the acquisition of something special — something we really wanted that would never be considered a casual or ordinary purchase. I can still remember how speechless I was when my parents presented me a low-end electric typewriter for my 14th birthday, because back in the olden days — the 1970s — one didn't just buy something because one wanted it, especially not something as luxurious as that.

My friend recalled how thrilled she was, at 15, with the "vanity package" her parents had given her; it included a lighted mirror, a blow dryer, and a curling iron. "Your typewriter, and my grooming supplies!" she marveled. "They were things you wanted and waited for. Now my kids tell me they want something, and somehow it becomes a 'need' — it's not even a treat; it's just something I go out and buy."

This, of course, is one of the pitfalls of prosperity: the more we have and the more readily we possess, the less we seek to possess God, and the more our spirits become distracted.

"The deceitful charms of prosperity destroy more souls than all the scourges of adversity," warned St. Bernard of Clairvaux.

We "treat ourselves" all the time, and because we do, we have become so expert at rationalizations that they take no energy at all:

- "I'm stopping off for a drink with the girls before I head home, because my manager is a jerk, and I deserve it."
- "I know my smart phone is perfectly fine, but the new one is out and I want it, and I can give the old one to my kid (if she'll accept it) or even better, my mother, who will never buy one for herself!"
- "The scale shows I'm down four pounds, so I can have ice cream because I'm sad today."

We can make excuses for ourselves *ad nauseam*, and when we do we are not only affecting our world, our families, our jobs, or our health; we are impacting our spirits too — and not in positive ways.

Permissiveness in parenting raises untrained, wild children who are constantly trying to gauge the lines; they do not understand the idea of boundaries. A daily habit of treating oneself creates a similar disorientation in adults as well. Benedictine monks and nuns will tell you, "Allow one fault and you will get another." By this, they don't mean we should be neurotic and over-scrupulous — as though our salvation depends upon our self-willed perfection (an idea that completely disrespects the workings of grace); rather, they mean that we must avoid becoming complacent about what permissions we give to ourselves. They mean we should maintain vigilance in honestly assessing our indulgence before it becomes a bad habit; otherwise, the boundaries become blurred and hard to discern.

Diminished perspective broadens our self-permissiveness, and excuses and rationalizations become easier and easier until, before we know it, our spiritual lives are sabotaged through our comfortable excuses and rationalizations. After a while, we don't even see our sins as actual sins; they become things we joke about:

- *Remember to keep holy the Lord's Day:* "C'mon, my job is demanding and the weekend is short and full of family obligations, and I'm sure I deserve to luxuriate on a Sunday morning, with coffee and the paper, instead of heading off to church. God already knows I love him, and he wants me to be happy, right?"
- *Thou shalt not steal:* "So, the clerk rang it up at the sale price, when it wasn't on sale. It's all right. It's probably going to be on sale next week. It all balances out, right?"
- *Thou shalt not commit adultery:* "It's a best-seller. So what if it's a little soft-porny? It's just a fantasy, and it spices things up — and what's wrong with that as long as I'm a good person?"
- *Thou shalt not take the name of the Lord thy God in vain:* "Oh, *madonna mi,* talk about being scrupulous! Why don't you kiss the goddamn floor over it, already?"

It is astounding how easy it is to rationalize our way out of grace and into sin. I confess to having permitted myself a sinful period of "small" but potent self-indulgence in my own life, by way of the *Catechism of the Catholic Church.* By exploiting a simple line on how maturity and psychological bearing contributed to some behaviors, and consequently impacted their moral weight and gravity, I rather masterfully (or madly, in retrospect) excused myself from self-accusation and conversion by recognizing that I was immature and psychologically deficient, which case I proved to myself (and eventually to a surprised priest) by suggesting that only someone immature and psychologically dented would grab a line from the *Catechism* in order to feel all right about her sinfulness, which was born of her immaturity and psychological woes.

The priest was so impressed with my creative rationalization that he gave me a creative penance and also ordered me to pray for an increase in vocations because "if more people start thinking like you, we're going to need a lot more priests!"

It is a prayer I keep up, even all these years later. A happy penance, actually.

So, is it a sin to "treat yo'self" once in a while? Of course not, as long as we understand — like Tom and Donna on *Parks and Recreation* — that we are "treating" ourselves, and that a "treat" is, by definition, something that is not a daily indulgence but a real occasion. For them — and for geeky, uptight Ben — the one-day excursion into extravagance actually became an opportunity for grace to work in their lives; the friends listened to each other and enjoyed each other in profound silliness that still had a point: when Ben admitted that buying a Batman suit would be an unthinkable "treat" for himself, he was not laughed at but encouraged. In the final scene, he signals with the snap of his Batcape that he has suddenly seen the value and gift of his nerdiness, and of all the small, unglamorous but helpful ways it serves those around him.

I know a family whose members scrupulously avoid desserts and snacks of any kind, except one Sunday a month, when they spread ice cream and cakes and goodies about the table and have "dessert for dinner"; grace abounds in that nutritionally suspect meal — which nobody misses — as the family relaxes and talks and laughs in each other's company, while "feasting" on what for too many of us have become such habitual pleasures that we no longer really enjoy them.

And that is the problem with too much self-treating, with the over-assuaging of our appetites, whether they originate in pride, gluttony, wrath, lust, sloth, envy, or greed. After a while, genuine regard is not enough; we need fawning sycophants. After a while, we don't even taste the chocolate; we just want more. After a while, it's not enough to indulge in our anger; we seek to destroy. After a while, we forget that the lust, or the jealousy, or the greed that has taken hold of our hearts and begun to own us, and to warp our perspectives, began with a small "treat" permitted without examination, without the recognition that we were, in fact, engaging in something unusual, and about which complacency could become deadly.

Allow one fault, and you permit another — and eventually, grace gets crowded out.

—

WHAT DOES CATHOLICISM SAY ABOUT SMALL INDULGENCES?

The repetition of sins — even venial ones — engenders vices, among which are the capital sins.
— Catechism of the Catholic Church (n. 1876)

We must take care of little faults: for he who once begins to go backward, and to make light of such defects, brings a sort of grossness over his conscience, and then goes wrong altogether.
— St. Philip Neri

Be gentle to all, and firm with yourself.
— St. Teresa of Ávila

Do not try to excuse your faults; try to correct them.

— St. John Bosco

Truly it is an evil to be full of faults; but it is a still greater evil to be full of them and to be unwilling to recognize them, since that is to add the further fault of a voluntary illusion.

— Blaise Pascal

A single bad book will be sufficient to cause the destruction of an entire monastery.

— St. Alphonsus Liguori

Self-control and strenuous effort curb desire; stillness and intense longing for God wither it.

— St. Thalassios the Libyan

—

HOW DO WE BREAK AWAY FROM THE SIN, OR HABIT, OF OVER-TREATING OURSELVES?

Take the advice of St. Philip Neri: One of the reasons you keep seeing his name pop up is because Philip Neri had a knack for giving great advice in succinct terms, and one thing he continually counseled visitors to his Oratory churches and his confessional was this: "Remember to read spiritual books, especially the Lives of the Saints":

> To get good from reading the Lives of the Saints, and other spiritual books, we ought not to read out of curiosity, or skimmingly, but with pauses; and when we feel ourselves warmed, we ought not to pass on, but to stop and follow up the spirit which is stirring in us, and when we feel it no longer then to pursue our reading.

What he is describing here is not simply reading about saints but using the examples of their lives, their own discoveries as they drew nearer to spiritual perfection, and their insights, as a kind of *lectio divina*, which means — simply put — to notice when you feel jolted or intrigued by something you have read, accept the feeling as a prompting of the Holy Spirit, and give yourself over to really thinking about the idea or biographical episode before you. Assume that the Holy Spirit wants you to glean an insight of your own, and readily consent to give yourself over to it. Re-read the passage aloud if you can, even if you must whisper the words, and then invite the saint to teach you what they know.

Be willing to let your imagination travel into it. Perhaps try breaking the idea down into a scene, or a dialogue, or even a haiku or a simple song. The point being, if your attention is being pulled toward a specific line, then do not read forward; rather, allow yourself to linger there, and to be led. In doing so, you will better commit what you've read to memory — if not word-for-word, at least in essences — and then you will be able to revisit what has intrigued you whenever you like, and continue to learn from it.

Researching the life of the great Benedictine abbess and mystic (and doctor of the Church) Hildegard of Bingen, I read her words, "Thus am I 'a feather on the breath of God,' " and became entranced at so delightful an image: imagine being a feather, blown about by God — it would mean surrender to God's will, of course, an idea I had often found (and sometimes still do find) challenging, and for the same reasons you probably do: What if God's will is something I really, really don't want, like illness, financial hardship, or untimely death? Hildegard's words were pretty, but just beneath them lay the reality of Christ Jesus at Gethsemane — and who among us really wants Gethsemane?

But thinking of it further — imagining a feather blown here and there, up and down — what struck me was the lightness of it all: lightness of flight, lightness of descent, lightness of landing.

A feather can be strewn about in the harshest of winds, and yet it remains light; it touches down lightly. Hildegard was saying that beyond being obedient to God's will, she was so confident that any event through which she was led was to her ultimate good, that she could bear all things with lightness; no grimacing. Therefore, because God is Good, only good can arise from our living within his slipstream, even if it looks ominous. It is a message we have heard before: Jesus tells us his yoke is easy and his burden is light. Hildegard's image spells it out in a remarkably accessible and beguiling way; subjecting it to a bit of *lectio* has helped me to remember it, and ponder it at challenging moments. In a prayer journal written several years after reading her words, I found myself writing, "O Love, keep me faithful, sustained by your lift — your air-dancer moving in time." It was a prayer directly informed by Hildegard — and yes, prayer journals can sometimes get very romantic like that.

Don't judge. Just go with the flow!

Reading the lives of the saints will inform your perspective and provide models of behavior that can help you learn about detachment from everything that is not God's will for you, and that would include the tendencies toward excessive self-indulgence that can ultimately pull you away from the spiritual practices that keep you grounded and open to grace. It won't happen overnight — I am proof of that — but in the course of time, little by little, saint by saint, *lectio* by *lectio,* and sometimes decade by decade, the desire to "treat yo'self" changes in subtle ways, until nothing feels like a better treat than doing something generous for someone else, instead of for yourself.

BE MINDFUL OF YOUR GUARDIAN ANGEL: Despite the brief angel craze of the 1990s, very few people really take their guardian angel seriously, but they are an ever-faithful source of assistance, if we will only remember to ask for their help. I have lately learned to talk to my guardian angel every day — I ask for help with my prayer (especially with the Rosary. If I am tired, I will begin by asking my angel to pray it with me, and complete it for me if I fall asleep). I ask my angel to please meet up with the guardian angel of those I will be meeting with later, especially if there is contention between us. I ask my angel to assist the angels of those I love, if they are in difficult or dangerous circumstances. I also ask my angel to be with me when I am feeling tempted to sin, to pray for me and uphold me — and if I'm really feeling like I am going to fall, to do battle with the tempter who has ensnared me.

I will confess that I do not always ask my angel to help me to avoid sin, but those are always times when — being perfectly honest here — I want to indulge my sin, and I fully intend to sin. I don't avail myself of the assistance that is mine for the asking, because I know it will come; my angel will come to my aid, and I will probably not get to do the thing I know I shouldn't do but want to do so badly. I choose poorly.

We forget how awful grave sin can feel until we give ourselves permission to indulge in it. We stupid, broken humans do that, sometimes; it is the very definition of mortal sin: to willfully give oneself over to the thing we know we should not want, and thus pull ourselves away from grace.

It is always a regrettable thing. It is always a refrain-from-the Eucharist-and-go-to-confession event, when I prefer my own desires over the help of my angel. After a while, one can't even plead immaturity or psychological deficiency; it's simply a desire for disorder, a consent to the agent of chaos and a reach back to original sin.

I am forever thanking my guardian angel for the help I know I am given. Sadly, sometimes I must also apologize for the help I have refused.

PRAY
(THIS PRAYER OR YOUR OWN)

Lord, you have given us a world full of so many good things, and through the example of your saints we know that all things, in moderation, exemplify your goodness. Help us to discern when we have begun to slide from occasional self-indulgences into habits that can render us so vulnerable to our cravings and desires — for food, for disordered fantasy, for success, for acceptance — that we begin to move away from you, and the gift of your grace. In the name of Christ Jesus. Amen.

CHAPTER FIVE

Gossip

That soul betraying so-and-so, the devil's radio.
— George Harrison

Harrison had it so right. *Gossip*. It's not only the devil's radio but his hobby as well. The word itself announces its low and slithering nature with a hiss. *Psst* mimics nothing so well as the flick of a serpent's tongue.

Psst. "Did you hear about...."
Psst. "Well, I heard...."

Can you hear it?

Psst. "So, did you hear about Kim Kardashian's latest publicity stunt?"
Psst. "Did you see how hideous she looked?"
Psst. "How can someone with that much money — and stylists and designers at the ready — look so awful, so often?"
Flick: "Man, if I had a third of her money, and privilege, I'd never leave the house looking like that!"

The hiss and then the flick — they are twin components of gossip: the *hiss* gets attention, and the *flick* releases a toxic venom that resides within us; its release makes us feel so much better —

for an instant, at least — because in the moment of the *flick*, we connect to the people who agree with us. In our validated concurrence, we also feel superior to the people we are talking about, who — if we are lucky — never find out that we have bared our fangs about them to others, in order to go *hiss*, and *flick*.

It's a funny thing about that venom, though. If its deployment is discovered, then its toxicity seems to deepen; its wounds become spread out, and lasting. But even if the object of our *psst*ing never knows that we struck, somehow the poison redounds back upon us anyway, and shrivels our souls just a little more. Why? Because gossip — slitherer that it is — slinks its way through the deadly sins, and pride, and wrath, and envy stick to it (and perhaps, sometimes, even the other four as well), and then we're carrying an awful lot of spiritual sickness with us.

Talk about toxicity! Gossip dehumanizes the people we're talking about by selling their dignity for a few cheap, ego-puffing observations; it dehumanizes us, for the purchase.

We all do it. We all engage in some measure of gossip, and most of the time we don't even realize we're doing it. We think we're simply being social. We're gabbing with friends, shooting the breeze, and it seems perfectly harmless, especially if we're gossiping about people we don't actually know and whose very public lives make them seem like fair game: first, for our attention, and then for our judgment. I'm pretty sure that those words about Kardashian (or words just like them) have appeared on my blog.

But Kardashian *wants* to be noticed and talked about, so it's not really gossip, is it? It's not the same as talking about a co-worker who is trying to hide that he's wearing a stained shirt because he can't afford a new one; it's not the same as whispering about the woman next door who looks like hell because that's where life has brought her. That's the sinful sort of gossip that dehumanizes both subject and gossiper, right? The Kardashians of the world want the attention, so where is the sin in giving it to them?

As I pondered this chapter I was startled to find myself coming back to Kim Kardashian, again and again. This is unusual; I do not follow her exploits unless they are thrust before me. But if you're preparing to talk about talking about people, it stands to reason that one of the most talked-about persons on the planet — someone who doesn't simply consent to be talked about but has pursued your notice, and your gossip, with a singularly dauntless energy — would keep popping into your awareness. Gossip is the whole perceived point of her public persona: *Look at me; now talk about me. Presto, I am famous, darlings!*

I've begun to appreciate Kardashian's shtick, because it's actually very shrewd (and yes, a little cynical). She identified a market that is both inexhaustible and never glutted: plain old *gossip*. People love to gossip, and that's never not true. The potential market for gossip is infinite. Pop stars may have a two-year shelf life, and styles and trends tire, season by season, but gossip is always in demand. Knowing this, Kardashian has tapped into and mined herself, offering to the public participation and shares in a rich vein of vamp and vanity that will take decades to deplete. She has traded on herself like a commodity, and the public — and the advertisers and media products that hope to attract them — has bought it up.

In exploiting what she knows about human nature, Kardashian created a product — namely, herself — and then marketed it relentlessly, and people responded because gossip is like the dessert table at an Italian wedding: people know they shouldn't indulge, but it's there, and it's free, so they wolf it down (maybe gossip has a gluttonous component after all), and Kardashian serves it up on heaping platters.

And here is what, perhaps, makes gossiping about someone like Kim Kardashian different from gossiping about the co-worker down the hall or your neighbor next door: Kardashian doesn't wear a dress with a falling hem and a rip in the bosom because she is poor; she doesn't wear it because she was on a bender the night before; she doesn't wear it because she feels fully beaten down by life and has given up. She wears it because she knows exactly what we will say about it. She invites gossip into her own luxury car and then drives where she wants it to go. She completely controls the narrative — and because that's true, it very likely touches her *not at all*. So yeah, our gossip and our judgments, our *pssts* and *flicks*, don't land anywhere near Ms. Kardashian.

That means, the poison is all on us, and in us. The gossip makes her richer, and more secure. It has precisely the opposite effect on us, because gossip, whether the subject seems to be fair game or not, always diminishes the gossiper; that is the constant.

Pope Francis is sometimes accused of speaking too ambiguously, but he has spoken often on gossip, and always with tremendous directness and clarity. The first time he addressed it came only a month into his papacy, in March 2013, and what he said has really stayed with me, because it was so perfectly and poetically put:

> I don't know why, but there is a dark joy in gossiping. Sometimes we begin by saying nice things about another, but then we slip into gossip, making the object of our chatter merchandise to be bartered. Let us ask forgiveness because when we do this to a friend, we do it to Jesus, because Jesus is in this friend.[2]

That was it: the "dark joy of gossip." Those words resonated with me, and to such an extent that often, when talking with friends, I will get a sense of things veering into the gratuitous and gossipy — usually around the time I notice that we all start to laugh at each other's snarky comments about another — and I will try to find the off-ramp by saying, "We've talked a lot about this person; let's pray for him." I have a good friend, who was also struck deeply by the words "dark joy," and on the rare occasions when our support for each other becomes a gripe session, one or the other of us will usually say, "This is starting to feel like dark joy," and we'll call it a night.

Dark joy is a perversion of real joy, which should always be light and bear light as well. Indulging in it only invites us to continue to seek out joy in dark places. What makes gossip joyful is the sense of superiority it gives us over another. We lose sight of our own flaws. We lose our own humility and build ourselves up in the creation of an "other," and then — though we may well hate ourselves in a million different ways — at least we're not like him or her. Because this is true, gossip always carries with it an undertone of *judgmentalism*. But as Pope Francis and countless saints down the ages have reminded us, we are meant to see and serve the Christ Jesus that resides within each of us. The very same Jesus, who was ridiculed and gossiped about (and judged) around the courtyard fire, and amid the palaces of Herod and Pilate, resides within the subject of our *psst*, and that is what makes gossip darker than we have ever imagined. We *psst*, and it is in the direction of Christ, and goodness and evil are face-to-face once again, as at Eden, as in the desert of temptations. In this encounter, however, the role of the serpent is being played by you, and by me.

Shortly after Francis made his observation about "dark joy," I got to watch it play out in real time between friends of mine, on Facebook. One of them, a priest with what I would call "moderately conservative" leanings, mentioned that while he liked what he was hearing from the new pontiff, he was not wholly on board with the universal acclaim Francis was receiving, particularly as so much of it seemed to come with ungenerous (and often erroneous) comparisons to his predecessor, Pope Benedict XVI. Others, who had not particularly admired Pope Benedict, were gobsmacked that anyone of any sense, any education, possessing any taste or refined sensibilities, would not immediately and in all ways prefer Francis. From my spy desk, I watched these people — all of whom I knew personally and professionally and liked very much — begin to talk about this extremely well-educated priest as though he was a nincompoop. They jeered at his "flyover country mentality" and his "narrow" and "elderly" point of view. As I watched the growing thread of smug derision, I saw perfectly Pope Francis' "dark joy" of gossip: social, agreeable, sometimes witty (or not), self-satisfied, and self-reassuring. Distilled down to basics, what this group was saying about the priest, and about themselves, was this:

• What a *maroon*! Typical reactionary conservative!
• And a dweeb.
• He is not like us.
• We are better than him.
• Our tribe is better than theirs.

At bottom, it was tribalism — the sort of immature bullying common to the playground, only playing out in the ether. I joined their conversation, remarking on how much I appreciated Francis' remarks on gossip and dark joy, and wondering how much anyone's theoretical admiration for the new pope counted if his words were not making genuine inroads into our thinking. I suggested that rather than saying amongst themselves, "Doesn't he realize ..." and "Does he think ..." they ought to go engage the priest and really try to hear his thoughts. They weren't actually interested in that, though. Their minds were already made up about Francis, and about this guy, who "just needed to get over" his concerns (which, eventually, he did) because Benedict was a l-o-s-e-r, and good riddance.

That Benedict's astonishing humility and trust in the Holy Spirit was responsible for Pope Francis never seemed to occur to them, except in the abstract; but then, that is a fact — and a continuum — that has sadly eluded many, particularly as they have filtered their thinking through the devil's own radio.

—

WHAT DOES CATHOLICISM SAY ABOUT GOSSIP?

Respect for the reputation of persons forbids every attitude and word likely to cause them unjust injury.[3] He becomes guilty:
— of *rash judgment* who, even tacitly, assumes as true, without sufficient foundation, the moral fault of a neighbor;
— of *detraction* who, without objectively valid reason, discloses another's faults and failings to persons who did not know them;[4]
— of *calumny* who, by remarks contrary to the truth, harms the reputation of others and gives occasion for false judgments concerning them.
— CATECHISM OF THE CATHOLIC CHURCH
(N. 2477, EMPHASIS IN ORIGINAL)

Detraction and calumny destroy the *reputation and honor of one's neighbor*. Honor is the social witness given to human dignity, and everyone enjoys a natural right to the honor of his name and reputation and to respect. Thus, detraction and calumny offend against the virtues of justice and charity.
— CATECHISM OF THE CATHOLIC CHURCH (N. 2479, EMPHASIS IN ORIGINAL)

Gossip always has a criminal side to it. There is no such thing as innocent gossip.... Some may say that there are persons who deserve being gossiped about. But it is not so.
— POPE FRANCIS (HOMILY, SEPTEMBER 13, 2013)[5]

When you hear ill of anyone, refute the accusation if you can in justice do so; if not, apologize for the accused on account of his intentions ... and thus gently check the conversation, and if you can, mention something else favorable to the accused.
— ST. FRANCIS DE SALES, *INTRODUCTION TO THE DEVOUT LIFE*

If something uncharitable is said in your presence,
either speak in favor of the absent, or withdraw,
or if possible, stop the conversation.
— St. John Vianney

If you cannot be merciful, at least speak as though you are a sinner.
If you are not a peacemaker, at least do not be a troublemaker.
If you cannot be assiduous, at least in your thought be like a
sluggard. If you are not victorious, do not exalt yourself over the
vanquished. If you cannot close the mouth of a man who disparages
his companion, at least refrain from joining him in this.
— St. Isaac of Syria

If you share secretly in the joy of someone you envy, you will be
freed from your jealousy; and you will also be freed from your
jealousy if you keep silent about the person you envy.
— St. Thalassios the Libyan

—

HOW DO WE BREAK AWAY FROM THE HABITUAL SIN OF GOSSIP?

ASK YOUR GUARDIAN ANGEL TO KEEP YOU FROM THE SIN OF GOSSIP BY
PROMPTING YOUR AWARENESS: Once you enlist the help of your angel, your awareness will immediately be heightened. If you really
can't keep yourself from thinking evil thoughts about another —
and yes, dark joy is evil — then ask your guardian angel to bring
your weakness directly to the Throne of the Almighty, in a plea for
merciful grace upon both you and the subject of your ire.

LEARN TO RECOGNIZE GOSSIP WHEN IT SHOWS UP:

- In business or social venues, discussions often segue into gossip, quite naturally and unintentionally. I once sat in an editorial meeting where a writer's name came up and an objection

was made to a piece he'd written. What began as a legitimate analysis of real weaknesses in his prose began to slip into joshing about his previous work, and before you knew it, his personal information was being bandied about quite casually. It's entirely possible that the man himself, if asked, might share some of that information, but none of us could know that. It was another "this is beginning to feel like 'dark joy' " moment for me, and one wherein I realized that gossip can sneak up on you. That might be its first characteristic.

- If talking about someone else's business makes you feel good; if it gives you a tingle of excitement, or somehow reassures you that you're really much better than the subject of your conversation, you might be gossiping. So ... if it feels good — but you're not actually discussing something good about another — then don't do it.

- Ask yourself, "Would I want someone talking about me in this way?" If the answer is no, you're probably gossiping.

Once you realize that you're engaging in gossip, stop: Just stop. Take the advice of the saints and try to turn the conversation toward positive things, or better yet, be bold enough to say, "Guys, this sounds like gossip. Let's move on." If it continues, and you can break away, you should try to.

Pray for the person or group you've gossiped about: There is no better way to sharpen your recognition of gossip, or to cultivate empathy for the subject of gossip, than to pray for him or her. Generally, once you empathize with people, you're much less inclined to gossip about them. Heck, once I came to appreciate Kim Kardashian's business plan, I couldn't indulge in laughing about her at all.

PRAY
(THIS PRAYER OR YOUR OWN)

Lord, in the days leading up to your passion, you were the subject of much gossip, which contributed to the sensibilities of the mob. Mob mentalities are never good, and too often gossip either arises from them or feeds them. Wishing no part of that mindlessness, nor to be party to any act that makes me barter away the humanity of another for my own amusement or validation — and wishing also to always remember that you are present in each of my fellows, I beg you, as did the psalmist, to "set a guard over my mouth and keep watch at the door of my lips" (see Ps 141:3), particularly when I am in the company of others and joining in casual talk, where discretion is too often lost. Shield me from my own thoughtlessness, I beg, in Christ's name. Amen.

CHAPTER SIX

Judgment and Suspicion

That's why I'm talking to you. You are one of the rare people who can separate your observation from your preconception. You see what is, where most people see what they expect.
— John Steinbeck, *East of Eden*

L ong ago, in our family, there resided a Mad Patriarch (MP) — a man who was not given at all to gossip, for the very good reason that he was already completely engaged with gossip's unattractive siblings, *judgment* and *suspicion*. While gossip might occasionally have "confirmed" this man's own warped thinking, it could contribute nothing substantive to his own ripe fantasies, one of which was that every woman between the ages of 8 and 62, and not currently located in a monastery or a grave, had only one thing on her mind, and it wasn't geometry.

In hindsight, I can generally (or eventually) consider pretty much everything that occurs to be a blessing — something I have learned from, or been formed by, or that placed me somewhere I might not have otherwise been, at precisely the right time. If it sometimes has felt like too many blessings made their appearance disguised as something else, I have learned that ready acceptance eventually reveals God's method in what sometimes can be mistaken for divine madness:

> Would to God that . . . all men could know how very easy it would be for them to arrive at a high degree of sanctity. They would only have to fulfill the simple duties of Chris-

tianity and of their state of life; to embrace with submission the crosses belonging to that state, and to submit with faith and love to the designs of Providence in all those things that have to be done or suffered.... This is the spirituality of all ages and of every state. (Jean-Pierre de Caussade, *Abandonment to Divine Providence*)

As concerns the MP, it was my misfortune to live in close quarters with him through my teenage years, and so my life — for the most part — went something like this:

- If I took care to style my hair, groom my nails, use a bit of lip gloss, and wear something that modestly suggested that I had a decent figure, I was clearly sweet on some boy; I was suspected of using my feminine wiles for the purpose of having sex.
- If I shaved my legs, I was suspected of wanting to have sex with somebody. Why would I shave my legs if I wasn't planning to give someone access to them? (A question for the ages!)
- If I wanted to accept an invitation to a party — where there might be both females and males in attendance — I was suspected of trying to be a social butterfly, who was either going to be raped by numerous young men, or was planning on freely giving myself to them.
- If I wanted to be anywhere but at home — someplace where there might be men who were not family members — I was just looking for trouble, and for a chance to shame the family.

Believe it or not, I was not raised in Saudi Arabia.

If I did none of those things — if I wore comfortable, less-fitted clothes and went without makeup, and did not shave my legs — and if I only hung out with my close girlfriends, I was accused of being a secret lesbian, and of course my two very girly friends were lesbians as well.

No matter what the circumstance, or my appearance, I was judged to be absolutely nothing more than a biological container enslaved to hormones and human sexual desire, and utterly out for ruin. Talk about not seeing the humanity of a person, or reducing a person to a kind of unit! This was very evil. Nuts, too.

Denials were futile, of course. If I was low-key in my defense, I was clearly both ashamed and disrespectful. A too-spirited defense, on the other hand, only proved my guilt, because expending excessive energy to deny an accusation based on nothing but suspicion and madness was evidence of a panicked guilt. Or something. I never did quite figure that one out; I only knew that if I strenuously objected to accusations that I was living in a state of perpetual hyper-licentiousness, my objections were all the proof that was needed.

Don't try to figure it out: living with a psychopath means never being able to sensibly square a circle, or still a whirling vortex. Suffice to say, being a social teenager became way too much work for me, so I spent most Saturday nights at home, cooking supper for the bosses and watching Lawrence Welk.

Music was a huge outlet and escape for me, but a college scholarship to study vocal performance had to be refused, because the professor who was urging me to accept it clearly only had one thing on his mind. I was too beaten down, and alone in my fight, to keep it up.

When it was discovered that I was communicating with a monastery to discern whether I had a religious vocation, I was suddenly considered (along with all nuns, it goes without saying) "warped and disordered."

When I smart-mouthedly suggested that I might, in fact, join the Navy, the MP roared as usual, but he was at least consoled by the fact that I was trending once again toward a lust-based life choice, rather than freakish celibacy. This, at least, could be understood. This, at least, contained a measure of normalcy, given that insatiable lust was humanity's default state.

There is a reason I finally simply left. Better to live within the jaws of a lion than to remain where I was. It was so much easier to be poor and on my own, scrambling for any job I could get in New York City, than to continue to live amid that insanity.

I share all of this not to seek out sympathy but as a means of demonstrating how difficult it is for people to deal in good faith with us when we allow our suspicions to guide our thinking, because every suspicion seeks its own validation, and this opens the pathway to judgment. Casting a suspicious eye upon others is a habit that grows naturally from a lazy garden of cynicism and negativity; judgmentalism is its attractive-looking-but-poisonous fruit.

This is not to say we ought never be suspicious about anyone; on the contrary, sometimes suspicion is warranted and even healthy. But how do we discern that?

Well, we possess intuition, and we also are able — if we are even remotely attentive to the people in our lives — to process patterns of behavior and to note, even subconsciously, when there is deviation from norms. If your child is usually cheerful and attentive and she suddenly becomes sullen and closed, it would be both normal and healthy — in fact, it is downright wise — to suspect that something is wrong; something has happened; something new has begun, has gone unshared, and must be found out.

Likewise — and I know this is a cliché and a stereotype, and I apologize to all of the honest salespeople out there, but clichés and stereotypes have some slight basis in reality — if you're looking at a used car, and your gut is telling you not to trust the salesman, he ought not be dealt with.

People who have been fooled, bullied, or hurt by people in their lives tend to have pretty good antennae about who not to trust. It's a self-protective instinct; if one is to err, one would prefer to err on the side of distrust, and at least get through the day relatively unscathed. That sort of suspicion is understandable, but if we give in to it too often, a sense of balance is lost. Sometimes, a chance must be taken, or one's highly developed sense of suspicion, taken into overdrive, will not allow room to work or argue in good faith.

As usual, I'm a living, breathing specimen of this habitual little sin, so I'll use myself as an example here. A family member once asked my husband and me (really, my husband) to check out a used car she was interested in. When we arrived at the dealership, I very quickly judged the salesperson to be shady. He seemed to know it too; he was constantly trying to distract me away from where he was, and I didn't want to go. Eventually — as they observed behavior from me they knew would involve a confrontation of sorts (imagine a bull, with steam coming from ears and nose as he paws the ground and lowers his head) — they sent me away to the other side of the car lot, but not before I hissed, "This guy is a crook," to them.

So, they bought the car, and the guy really was a crook; when the car had trouble within the 30-day warranty, he tried to shine-on my tenacious family member until she got the repairs she was due. This event, and a few subsequent repairs later, caused me to unattractively repeat, "I knew he was a crook and a shyster. I told you! You guys never listen to my gut!"

Finally, my husband pointed out that my gut has so predictable a habit of looking for (and snap-judging) the snakes lying in our social grasses that it sometimes needs to be put in its place, and this car purchase had seemed like one of those times. "Sometimes your gut takes a psychopathic left turn," he said, "and then no one wants to listen to you."

"It didn't that time!" I snorted.

"No, not this time," he agreed. "But your suspicion was so fast and so furious, that it was off-putting, and that made it easy to put aside."

So, the moral of that story is: yes, your gut does sometimes lead you into suspicious judgments that are valid, so don't ignore it. But on the other hand, if you're habitually looking at the world with a jaundiced eye, suspecting everyone all the time, your credibility will be damaged. And someone will pay for that damage in the form of a lemony car, because no one trusts you anymore.

The flip side of that, of course, is that a too-suspicious nature can terribly wrong a person, as I was wronged by the Mad Patriarch. I've been guilty of that too, although not to his dramatic degree. Still, I've managed to think the worst of someone only to be proven very wrong, and in doing so I've had to apologize to the person, and also acknowledge to myself (and my confessor) that I had once again looked at a human being and seen only a unit — something that contained categories of possible deceit — and had not been able to give him or her the benefit of a doubt. In doing so, I had injured that person and revealed my own foolishness and deficiencies as well.

When we see people only as units of possible harm, threat, or sin, we are connecting ourselves to wrath, and often to pride as well — again, we're feeding on the by-products of the deadly sins. And Jesus — who was suspected by some of having political ambitions, and judged a failure by those who hoped those suspicions were true — had a lot to say about judgment, well beyond "let who is without sin cast the first stone."

In Matthew's Gospel he says: "Judge not, that you be not judged. For with the judgment you pronounce you will be judged, and the measure you give will be the measure you get" (Mt 7:1-2, RSV).

I often think about that and then offer up a prayer for the soul of the Mad Patriarch; I wouldn't wish his judgments to be thrown back at him, because they were heinous. Likewise, if we are stopped at a red light and we see someone who seems to us "suspicious enough" to make us check that our doors are locked (thereby rendering a judgment upon that person that may be utterly unfair), do we want to have that sense of being unseen for ourselves, of being unknown-yet-judged, come back to us?

We do this as a society all the time. We look at people of another race and immediately form ideas about them that lead to judgments informed by nothing, and yet go bubbling up into our psyche and down into our hearts and souls. We see someone with multiple piercings and tattoos and our antennae vibrate wildly. We see someone with a crew cut and a pickup truck and it happens again.

We see a man or a woman and, based solely on their gender, suspect them of ambitions they may not possess.

We meet a homosexual person, a transgendered person, or anyone falling within the ever-growing alphabet-frames of 21st-century sexuality, and we quickly assume things about them, or suspect things about their background, and then judge them.

At our absolute worst, our assumptions, suspicions, and judgments become presumptuously concerned with how fit this or that person might be for heaven, or where he or she falls on the morality scale. And, oh heavens, having been an innocent suspect, having been judged like that, I surely don't want that sort of judgment to redound to me!

It's all about projection, in the end. When we give in to our suspicions about other people, we don't realize that they arise from ourselves — the suspicions we harbor about others are, very often, culled from our own shriveled souls; we project onto them the very thing *we* would do. Thus, with too many of our suspicions and judgments against other people, we indict ourselves. And then we're very much going to need the abundant mercy that Jesus describes in Luke's Gospel:

> "Judge not, and you will not be judged; condemn not, and you will not be condemned; forgive, and you will be forgiven; give, and it will be given to you; good measure, pressed down, shaken together, running over, will be put into your lap. For the measure you give will be the measure you get back." (Lk 6:37-38, RSV)

In the first century, those listening to Jesus would have understood the fullness of recompense he was describing: oils or grains pressed down, blended together to ensure a uniformity of quality — their measurement "running over" in order that the quantity might not be shorted. So all of our sins will be blended, shaken together, perhaps, with how we have been sinned against. And all of our mercies will be measured to overflowing so that their proper accounting may be ensured.

—

WHAT DOES CATHOLICISM SAY ABOUT SUSPICION AND JUDGMENT?

To avoid rash judgment, everyone should be careful to interpret insofar as possible his neighbor's thoughts, words, and deeds in a favorable way:

Every good Christian ought to be more ready to give a favorable interpretation to another's statement than to condemn it. But if he cannot do so, let him ask how the other understands it. And if the latter understands it badly, let the former correct him with love. If that does not suffice, let the Christian try all suitable ways to bring the other to a correct interpretation so that he may be saved.[6]
— CATECHISM OF THE CATHOLIC CHURCH (N. 2478)

It is the Lord, it is Jesus, Who is my judge. Therefore I will try always to think leniently of others, that He may judge me leniently, or rather not at all, since He says: "Judge not, and ye shall not be judged."
— ST. THÉRÈSE OF LISIEUX, STORY OF A SOUL

Criticism of others is thus an oblique form of self-commendation. We think we make the picture hang straight on our wall by telling our neighbors that all his pictures are crooked.
— ARCHBISHOP FULTON J. SHEEN, SEVEN WORDS OF JESUS AND MARY: LESSONS ON CANA AND CALVARY

He who busies himself with the sins of others, or judges
his brother on suspicion, has not yet even begun to repent
or to examine himself so as to discover his own sins.
— ST. MAXIMOS THE CONFESSOR, ON LOVE (N. 55)

If you don't behave as you believe, you will end by
believing as you behave.
— ARCHBISHOP FULTON J. SHEEN

In prayer and in every work of your life avoid suspiciousness,
doubt, and diabolical imaginations. Let your spiritual eye
be single, in order that the whole body of your prayer,
of your works and of your life may be light.
— ST. JOHN OF KRONSTADT, MY LIFE IN CHRIST (PART II)

———

HOW DO WE BREAK AWAY FROM THE HABIT OF SUSPICION AND THE SIN OF JUDGMENT?

RECALL A TIME WHEN SOMEONE JUDGED YOU BEFORE KNOWING YOUR STORY: Remember how it felt when someone suspected you unfairly, or how it scalded to realize that someone presumed to know anything about you that you had not yourself revealed to them? Why would you want anyone to ever feel that way?

Now, recall a time when your own suspicions and judgments ran wild. Sometimes they may have been justified. But what happened when they were not? How much were you responsible for hurting someone else? How much did it humiliate you to realize that your suspicions brought you to low places, instead of the higher ones?

VOLUNTEER, SOMEWHERE: That may sound like it's coming out of left field, but in truth, when we volunteer to help out in a hospital, our parish, or elsewhere, we are stretched out of our comfort zones and introduced to a broader variety of people than which we might usually associate. This is a good way to learn to limit knee-jerk suspicions. Volunteering in the pastoral-care office of a hospital, I found myself wandering into the rooms of patients whose lives were so completely different than my own that it left me recalibrating everything I thought I knew (or had been conditioned to think) about all sorts of people. It made my life better and made me a better person too. In the end, I'm quite sure my volunteerism ended up benefiting me more than anyone I might have helped.

PRAY
(THIS PRAYER OR YOUR OWN)

Eternal God, you have made it clear that there is such a thing as judgment, but that it rightly belongs to your Son, Christ Jesus, to whom you have given it (Jn 5:22). Help me to be ever mindful that when I allow my suspicions to become charged, I am running headlong into the temptation to judge and then to condemn. In doing so, I am presuming against Christ, and also failing to see the human being before me, beyond what I really want and prefer to see. Teach me to look at my fellows with eyes infused with a measure of your compassion and love, that I might one day enjoy a mercy "pressed down, shaken together, running over." Most emphatically, I beg that at my culmination, no one will ever look back upon my life and describe me to others as a "Mad Patriarch/ Matriarch." In Christ's name, have mercy upon us all. Amen.

CHAPTER SEVEN

Gloominess and Griping

*Well, if there's a bright center to the universe,
you're on the planet that it's farthest from.*
— Luke Skywalker, *Star Wars: A New Hope*

M y mother resided on one of those dark planets. Over the years, I've come to appreciate both the lunacy and the sorrow that launched her toward it, and this appreciation colors my memories of her with a kind of rueful humor. In truth, in the 20 years since her death, I've felt closer to her than I ever did in life, especially when I recognize in myself some of her habitual gripes and grouchy expressions emanating from my own mouth.

One of my strangest memories is of my mother telling me to make sure she was buried with her Communion pin and prayer book, and that if I forgot, she would come back to haunt me.

I was four years old at the time.

Even at that tender age, I accepted that people and pets lived and died, but I hadn't yet worked out that "people" included my parents. That reality struck me as I sat on the basement steps, one afternoon, watching my father play the piano. He was a very fine musician, but — owing to a disagreement between his own parents as to whether he should learn the piano or the violin — he never studied and couldn't read a note of music. This deficiency accorded him a measure of humiliation all his life and kept him from calling himself a musician, but he could play any instrument he picked up and was particularly impressive at the keyboard.

Watching him play that afternoon, I sensed the joy he took in making music, and I think I also sensed his melancholy. In that moment, at that young age, I had no way of expressing an interior knowledge so secret and so harsh — that music would forever entrap him within a dichotomy of pleasure and pain.

Unable to articulate it, all I could do was bawl. I watched him play, understood something for which I had no words, and — deciding that it all had something to do with love and death — became incredibly emotional; I worked myself up into a fine hysterical frenzy that scared my father's hands from the keyboard and sent my mother running, demanding to know what was the matter.

"I don't want Daddy to die!" I wailed and gasped. "And I don't want you to die!"

"We're not dying!"

That meant nothing to me. I was howling by now, and beginning to hyperventilate. I pronounced sentence upon my parents, as my lungs burned scarlet: "But you will, someday! Someday you're both going to die!"

My mother, way out of her league in terms of consolation, and looking for anything she could use to put an end to my disordered freak, said, "You gotta stop thinking about it; it's bad for your veins!"

Traditional Chinese medicine might coincidentally concur with her on that, but at the moment this was no help at all. Considering that someday my parents were going to die, and at any moment my veins might be collapsing, I let go another wail, at which point my father — no drinker but by now completely spooked — availed himself of a bit of Johnnie Walker Red. My mother, in the end, seemed somewhat reassured. After all, death (particularly her own) was one of her favorite topics, and so my sensibilities were doing her proud.

To a point, there is nothing wrong with that: the Church and her saints teach us that *memento mori* ("remember your death") is a valuable tool for habituating mindfulness in our lives. My mother used it more for entertainment purposes, coupling it with a taste for eschatology. Sometimes, as she poured my Rice Krispies before school, she would intone, "The world is going to end in the year 2000," and then float back to the coffeepot. My cereal would snap, crackle, and pop itself soggy as I did the math. *Crap.* I'd only be 42 years old. That didn't seem very fair.

But the truth is, life is not fair, at least not to our human understanding of fairness. As Christians, we know that "all things work to God's own purpose" — and God's purposes are always right and just — but we tend to forget all that in our day-to-day living. Perhaps beside *memento mori*, we should scribble *memento iustitia Deo* ("remember God is just") to help bring the point home. Then we might be less inclined toward the small habitual sins of gloominess and griping, which not only scare little children but also leave them — and all of us — wondering what the point of life is.

"We live out our hell on earth," my mother used to say. "That's what I think."

"What about the people in purgatory?" I once asked.

"Purgatory is for the people who didn't suffer enough on earth," she'd posit. "Everyone has to get their fair share of suffering." On that downer of a note, she'd give me something snacky to eat and send me outside to play. I would sit beneath a weeping willow tree, or within a cove of fragrant evergreens, and finger the soft moss and wonder how she could talk about "hell-on-earth" when there was so much heaven all around.

I was a good deal older before I realized that my mother had lived a hard and unsettled life, one so full of hard luck, instability, and violence that a philosophy of casual fatalism and nearly continual grousing seemed not only understandable but a reasonable sort of survival tactic. When the world is hard, one needs a shield, a way to say, "This touches me not," particularly if one has a sensitive nature. The more I learned about her childhood, and watched as her "bad luck" continued, the more I could accept that it all looked like hell to her.

Still, as an adult, I returned to her house to help her out as she recovered from a cancer surgery, and I began to wonder whether her constant negativity and perpetual griping hadn't contributed to her increasingly difficult health. Five days into my visit I heard myself saying, "Mom, for the love of God, say something positive!"

By day eight, I couldn't wait to get home.

The saddest part of this story is that I, too, find myself falling into a habit of gloom and grouchiness, only becoming aware of it when one of my sons rolls his eyes and echoes my words to my mother, back at me: "Woman, say something positive!" When I've really been going hard at it, they'll even call me by my mother's name, and then I am properly chagrined, especially because — having watched my parents — I know that it's one thing to indulge a fit of crabbiness, now and then, and another thing entirely to be so committed to seeing the downside of everything that you live your life like a curmudgeon, in a state of perpetual gloom and doom and botheration. The first is simply a symptom of our shared, and flawed, humanity. The second is a habit that can literally pull you away from heaven, long before you are ever headed there.

The very bad habit of grousing and glooming is an easy one to develop, because usually when we voice our miseries large and small, the people around us are not just sympathetic but in agreement. You walk into the office and everyone complains about the weather, or the boss, or the clients, or the lousy coffee; griping is a communal and social jumping-off point — it's the thing to say when there is nothing meaningful to say. People will join in on negative comments because everyone can relate.

Grousing is inclusive in a way sunny optimism cannot be, because while a day's pleasures may not be fully absorbed, all of us are conscious of its pinpricks.

A little grousing, a little complaining; again, one of those things we all do, and a small measure of it can be cathartic, even therapeutic. When it becomes our default mode of expression, however, we let it all become sinful. "What's there to be happy about, anyway?" an office mate used to ask, morosely, of the air.

For Christian people, quite a lot, actually, and I could fill pages extolling the good things of creation, the mercies of God, and the mysterious plans by which our genuine tragedies are often looked back upon and seen as workings which brought us to where we are — a place (spiritually or personally or professionally) we likely would not be at, by any other means.

Or, I could simply sing for you the entirety of Psalm 117, as I've memorized it:

> Praise the Lord, all you nations give praise.
> Extol him all people of God.
> For great is his love for us;
> and the faithfulness of the Lord never ends.
> Praise the name of the Lord.

It is so important to recognize this truth and to believe it: when we stop seeing and appreciating what is good, we are left only with what seems to us — often very justifiably — to be not good; to be bad. We abandon everything that hints of "yes" in our lives and attach ourselves to what feels like "no."

But God exists in "yes." God is Good. Christ Jesus himself says it: "Why do you call me good? No one is good but God alone" (Mk 10:18, RSV).

If nothing seems to be "good" in your life, then God cannot be alive in your heart and mind. If everything, to us, is always "bad," then we really do live a kind of hell on earth, because hell is where we take ourselves, in order to be away from God. Hell is the great nothingness, where God is not.

I know this chapter has been amusing in parts, and that sins of gloominess and grumps might make it seem pretty light-weight; but the truth is, the little sins we are discussing here are very heavy, and they put a great weight upon our souls. When we examine our complaints, or what has triggered our grouchiness and our increasing sense of there being a pall over our lives, we will usually discover that we're indulging some of the deadly sins, and that our indulgence of them has led us to engage in the rest of them:

- We complain because life seems unfair. Someone else has something good and we should have it as well, because we're as good as anyone. There's pride and envy.
- We grouse and become morose because life has been hard and no one seems to understand what we've been through, dammit! There's pride and wrath.
- Feeling unseen, unappreciated, unrewarded, we say "to hell with this" and enhance the trajectory. We give up, and thus entertain sloth. We try to swallow back the pride and wrath and envy, and we end up being gluttonous. We try to console ourselves with worldly appreciation and end up falling into lust and greed.

Truly, marinating in our gripes and complaints only softens us up for the evil one, who cheerfully helps us climb into quite a stewpot of our own miserable creation — and there we hide in the darkness, with a fire below, until we bubble down to nothing. Where God is not.

—

WHAT DOES CATHOLICISM SAY ABOUT GLOOMINESS, GRIPING, AND GROUCHES?

Do all things without grumbling or questioning, that you may be blameless and innocent, children of God without blemish in the midst of a crooked and perverse generation, among whom you shine as lights in the world, holding fast to the word of life.
— PHILIPPIANS 2:14-16 (RSV)

A cheerful heart is good medicine,
but a downcast spirit dries up the bones.
— PROVERBS 17:22 (RSV)

Count it all joy, my brethren, when you meet various trials, for you know that the testing of your faith produces steadfastness. And let steadfastness have its full effect, that you may be perfect and complete, lacking in nothing.
— JAMES 1:2-4 (RSV)

"You ask and do not receive, because you ask wrongly, to spend it on your passions."[7] If we ask with a divided heart, we are "adulterers";[8] God cannot answer us, for he desires our well-being, our life. "Or do you suppose that it is in vain that the scripture says, 'He yearns jealously over the spirit which he has made to dwell in us?' "[9] That our God is "jealous" for us is the sign of how true his love is. If we enter into the desire of his Spirit, we shall be heard.

Do not be troubled if you do not immediately receive from God what you ask him; for he desires to do something even greater for you, while you cling to him in prayer.[10]

God wills that our desire should be exercised in prayer, that we may be able to receive what he is prepared to give.[11]
— CATECHISM OF THE CATHOLIC CHURCH (N. 2737)

I must die to myself continually and accept trials without complaining. I work, I suffer, and I love with no other witness than his heart. Anyone who is not prepared to suffer all for the Beloved and to do his will in all things is not worthy of the sweet name of Friend, for here below, Love without suffering does not exist.

— ST. BERNADETTE SOUBIROUS (VISIONARY OF LOURDES)

In the same way that a powerful medicine cures an illness, so illness itself is a medicine to cure passion. And there is much profit of soul in bearing illness quietly and giving thanks to God.

— AMMA SYNCLETICA

When it is all over, you will not regret having suffered; rather you will regret having suffered so little, and suffered that little so badly.

— ST. SEBASTIAN VALFRÈ

God save us from gloomy saints!

— ST. TERESA OF ÁVILA

—

HOW DO WE BREAK AWAY FROM GLOOMINESS, GRIPING, AND GROUCHING?

CULTIVATE WHAT IS CALLED AN "ATTITUDE OF GRATITUDE": Grateful hearts do not fall into the sins we've been concerning ourselves with: griping, complaining, gossiping, judging, suspicion. A grateful heart, proverbs say, "maketh a merry countenance." It also acts as a shield against our own gift for wrapping ourselves up in gloom. If you need to make a list of things for which you are grateful, do that; every night, try to add one thing to it. After a while, you will be surprised at how long the list has grown, and what seemingly "negative" situations have contributed to it.

USE SHORT EJACULATORY PRAYERS TO BRING YOU TO MINDFULNESS:

- Stuck in traffic? "Thank you, Lord, that I have a car to help me travel about!"
- Nothing good on television? "Thank you, Lord, for this awful invention that brings me important information and allows our family to spend time together!"
- Too many repairs needed on your house? "Thank you, Lord, that we have this cruddy old house, when some must make do with a shack or a cardboard box."
- Facing a chronic illness? "Thank you, Lord, that I have this chance to join my sufferings to yours for the sake of the world."

STUDY THE OPENING VERSE OF JOHN'S GOSPEL, LINE BY LINE: It is a beautifully wrought piece of theology, containing the whole mystery of God and creation within its verses, which is why it can be pondered for a whole lifetime, and recited in times of stress to great effect. I am always reminded therein that God is in charge, that he has a plan, and that his plan is enshrouded in his ongoing and perpetual "YES," through which the universe is sustained and expanded. Most importantly, it reminds me that I do not wish to be within any part of the nothing:

> All things came to be through him,
>   and without him nothing *came to be*. (Jn 1:3, NAB)

Emphasis mine. Without God, nothing is created: both nothing, and nothingness itself. *Nothing* came to be, without God; where God was not.

It is one of those ripe and tantalizing mysteries worth diving into, especially as an exercise in *lectio divina*, but also as a means of looking at a troubling area of your life and locating where God may reside within it. There, we may find a place restful enough to dispel all of our gloominess and silence all of our grouses.

PRAY

(THIS PRAYER OR YOUR OWN)

Lord, we Christians have the image of your cross always before our eyes, and yet we seldom seem to truly take in its lessons. Let the crucifix of Christ Jesus serve to remind us, again and again, that there is nothing we undergo in life — no suffering, no mortification, no burden — that has not been known and shared by him. Help us to remember that we always have before us a choice: to engage with our lives with the common, earthly habit of complaining, and grousing, and the surrendering of hope, or to "offer up," in prayerful thanksgiving, those things we find to be irksome and difficult, joining them to Christ and the cross, in order to detach from them. In this way, they are also joined to you, in your heavenly kingdom, and we have given some small measure of affirmation and action to our own hopes to reside there with your saints. We ask this through your Son, Christ Jesus. Amen.

Chapter Eight

Deliberate Spite or Passive Aggression

Nobody really wants us. So let us watch and say jaggy things,
in the hope that some of them will hurt.
— J. M. Barrie, *Peter Pan*

I knew someone who often bragged about his talent for vengeance, which he described as "very satisfying."

"Do me wrong," he would say, "and I won't make a fuss at you; I won't cause a scene or call you out. But eventually, I will get you back, and I can be unbelievably patient while waiting for my chance."

At that point, those of us around him would hum the theme song from *The Godfather*, and he would laugh.

No one took him seriously, because no one had ever seen the hint of malicious intent about him, or seen him put action behind this philosophy of spiteful vengeance. All of his noise about vengeance was likely a cover for the fact that he was, in truth, very sensitive, very loving, and very easily hurt.

I need to reference my friend and his outsized claims, here, because on this issue — and about eight chapters and about 23,000 words into this thing — we have finally fallen upon a bad habit and "little sin" that does not come naturally to me, and for which my own life is not the primary cautionary tale. This is not because I am praiseworthy or particularly saintly about this *one* thing. It is simply because my sloth overrules my sense of payback; I simply don't have the energy for spite, or for its narrow-eyed, bullying cousin: passive-aggression.

"I'll get you back" is a primitive feeling, and we know that because it is behavior we see even among toddlers, who will instinctively knock down each other's sandcastles. Tellingly, though, once that happens, they often both end up crying; they share the tragedy. Neither of them feels happy, even though a supposed debt has been resolved.

Spite says, "I'll get you back" and "If I can't have this, you can't either," but it also says, "Now you know how I felt," and this is a clue to how pathetic it is when we allow ourselves to resort to spite in an effort to assuage our feelings and burnish our sense of justice. Its vengeance gives us a false assurance that not only have we made clear who we are, but that we have spelled out, very precisely, exactly that behavior up with which we will not put:

- "You hurt my feelings, so I am not speaking to you."
- "You embarrassed me in that meeting, so now I will make a mockery of you before everyone — and if you're not a good sport about it, you'll look even worse for not 'taking a joke.' "
- "You cheated on me, so I cheated on you. Now you know how I felt!"
- "If you try to boss me around, I will do exactly the opposite of what you tell me to do, or not to do."

We think we're creating boundaries, when in fact our sense of injury has us running a bit wild; when we are sane, we have no interest in actively seeking an opportunity to hurt someone else. Reasonable boundaries exist as much to remind us of what ground we prefer to inhabit as to tell others how far they may go. Too often, our need for payback goes far beyond what might be considered "fair," and leaves us inhabiting a barren place, and walking it alone.

A woman I know spent the first 25 years of her marriage "getting back" at her husband, and sometimes her kids, by not speaking to them. If she and her husband fought, or if she felt that one of the kids had disrespected her, she would simply go silent. She would still cook and clean and do everything as she normally would, but she would do it all in silence. She greeted no one, talked to no one, and listened to whatever anyone needed for school or church and then provided it to them, but she did it in a breathtakingly cold silence.

As a frequent visitor to the house, I once witnessed the family endure three weeks of silence from this woman. Being an insecure person who immediately assumed that cold or distant behavior was about me (and also my fault), I finally could take no more of it and asked her whether I had done something to offend her.

She seemed not just puzzled by the question but sincerely concerned that I would think such a thing.

"Well, you don't talk when I'm here," I explained. "I figured I had done something that bothered you."

It turned out that she was mad at her husband, who had called her a "big mouth" during an argument. As my visits usually coincided with his arrival home from work, I had simply been present to the daily freeze-out, which none of the kids had noticed, and which — it has to be said — didn't seem to have bothered her husband.

"But, it's been, like, three weeks," I said to her. "You haven't talked to your husband in three weeks because he called you a big mouth?"

"That's right. When someone makes me mad, I don't talk to them until I get an apology. I have my dignity!"

"I guess I get that," I said. "But what if he dies on the way to work? Aren't you going to feel terrible if, say, he gets killed on the job? You'll probably wish you could trade your dignity for a do-over of the last three weeks, then."

I wasn't intentionally being a smart-ass, but she took it that way — and officially stopped speaking to me too, but only for the rest of the night. The following day came the big thaw — both her husband and I were readmitted into her good graces — and for as long as I knew her, she never subjected anyone to the "silent treatment" again. Perhaps *memento mori* (or *memento mori sposa*) came into play, and getting a bit of her own back — or defending her dignity through spite, when a direct conversation would be a more productive way to go — began to seem too costly a bargain after all.

As ever, this "little sin" of holding a grudge until vengeance has been meted out, until the scales of justice seem re-balanced, has a great deal to do with the great sin of pride, and with our ego, and with our need to be seen and heard by others. In this woman's case, she had been wounded by her husband's words, and wanted to both punish him and force him to see her and value her, but she did it in the most passive way possible, with silence. By continuing to fulfill his material needs, she added an element of guilt to the whole endeavor: "Even though I am too angry and hurt to talk to you, I am still doing right by you," goes that merciless script, which strives to both punish and induce guilt. In so doing, it cannot help but lose sight of love, and the God who is All-Love, and in whose teaching about love there is no room for spite, or for malice, or for passive-aggressive worth-seeking.

No one is ever wrong for wanting to be fully seen, fully recognized, or fully valued, but the ways in which we seek out that recognition must be centered in authentic love, or else there will be perversion, and spite suits that perfectly.

Sometimes, if we cannot be direct in our spite and aggression, we become indirect, or we redirect it toward ourselves. I'm thinking of how many celebrated, famous people seem to get tripped up by their very success, and it's usually because, although they have become famous — meaning, their names are "known" — they themselves are not really *known* at all, not for themselves, and not by people who matter to them.

We routinely watch actors and musicians — whose genuine passion for their art has propelled them to the fame they thought they desired — crash and burn once their lives become full of strangers who "know" them, "love" them, but not authentically. Fomenting relationships, particularly after they have become famous — with those who would truly know them, truly love them, and truly see their personhood beyond the public persona — becomes the greatest challenge of their lives. They begin the cycle of self-spiting reckless behavior — the multiple marriages and stints in rehab — that has almost become a cliché for the price of fame. "You think you know me? You say you love me? Well, you weren't expecting this, were you? You sure can't love that, can you? I'm going to make myself as hard to love as possible, and force you to prove your love, or admit that I'm really nothing, and that you're a liar."

The pursuit for human understanding and intimacy is not evil, but it can result in behaviors that tempt evil, or develop a passing acquaintance with it. Ironically, this makes the authentic love we seek that much more difficult to recognize. Here, the wise words of an Orthodox priest, Father Alexander Schmemann, bear repeating: "Every evil screams out only one message: 'I am good!' And not only does it scream, but it also demands that the people cry out tirelessly in response: 'You are good, you are freedom, you are happiness.' " When behavior is calculated to wrench such a response from us, whether in apology or pity or remorse, there is always an element of spite or aggression somewhere within it.

If the man who bragged about his love of vengeance were serious, he could never have hidden it behind such consistent personal warmth; somewhere, there would have been destruction, because destruction is always the end result when love and justice are manipulated.

—

WHAT DOES CATHOLICISM SAY ABOUT
SPITEFUL BEHAVIOR OR PASSIVE AGGRESSION?

Let all bitterness and wrath and anger and clamor and slander
be put away from you, along with all malice.
— EPHESIANS 4:31 (RSV)

"You shall not take vengeance or bear any grudge
against the sons of your own people, but you shall love
your neighbor as yourself: I am the LORD."
— LEVITICUS 19:18 (RSV)

Do not say, "I will repay evil!"
Wait for the LORD, and he will help you.
— PROVERBS 20:22 (RSV)

Do not repay anyone evil for evil; be concerned for what is noble
in the sight of all. If possible, on your part, live at peace with all.
Beloved, do not look for revenge but leave room for the wrath; for
it is written, "Vengeance is mine, I will repay, says the Lord." Rather,
"if your enemy is hungry, feed him; if he is thirsty, give him something
to drink; for by so doing you will heap burning coals upon his head."
Do not be conquered by evil but conquer evil with good.
— ROMANS 12:17-21 (NAB)

Sin committed through malice, by deliberate
choice of evil, is the gravest.
— *CATECHISM OF THE CATHOLIC CHURCH* (N. 1860)

Pain is never permanent.
— ST. TERESA OF ÁVILA

If a man finds it very hard to forgive injuries, let him look at a
crucifix, and think that Christ has shed all His Blood for him, and not

only forgave his enemies, but prayed the Eternal Father
to forgive them also. Let him remember also that when he
says the *Pater Noster* every day, instead of asking pardon
for his sins, he is calling down vengeance upon them.
— ST. PHILIP NERI

Very often we act in the opposite manner: we add malice to malice
by our anger, we oppose pride with pride. Thus, evil grows within us
and does not decrease; it is not cured — rather it spreads.
— ST. JOHN OF KRONSTADT

God judged it better to bring good out of evil
than to suffer no evil to exist.
— ST. AUGUSTINE

The world is full of malice, and no prudence of vigilance
is sufficient to avoid being contaminated.
Only by fleeing from it can it be beaten.
— ST. PIO OF PIETRELCINA

—

HOW DO WE BREAK AWAY FROM HABITS OF SPITE, MALICE, AND PASSIVE AGGRESSION?

RESIST THE URGE TO PLAY GOD: Take a page from Hamlet's father's ghost. Murdered by his brother Claudius (who then took Hamlet's mother, Gertrude, for his queen), his father (who had plenty of encouragement toward spitefulness) tells Hamlet,

> Taint not thy mind, nor let thy soul contrive
> Against thy mother aught. Leave her to heaven
> And to those thorns that in her bosom lodge
> To prick and sting her.

In other words, "Kiss her up to God and the weight of her own conscience." It's perfect advice: when we are stung and our instinct to spite another or to seek some sort of passive-aggressive vengeance against them, refer them instead to God, who is All-Justice and knows far better than we the best way to deal with both our pain and theirs. Whether their own conscience can rein them in, or not, is actually not our concern at all.

CALL OUT YOUR EGO: Acknowledge quickly when your ego is prompting you to serve spitefulness, particularly if someone calls you out on it; they are, in a very real sense, the voice of heaven communicating with you.

Earlier in the chapter, I said that this is a sin to which I am not overly susceptible, and that is true for the most part. But my ego is as mad as anyone's — and yes, I got one of those callouts. My husband and I, and our grown children, were visiting an amusement park and — as my severely arthritic knees and spine were acting up — we rented one of those cool motor-driven chairs so that I could painlessly keep up with them. At one point, as they stopped to look at something, I continued forward, and when my husband called out for me to hang back, I resisted. Heady with the ease of my newfound mobility, I replied, "You're not the boss of me," and then deliberately moved farther ahead, before distracting myself by tracing a circular pattern on the ground. My daughter-in-law tagged me on it later, saying, "Really? '*You're not the boss of me*'? Like you're five?"

It took a few years for me to gain enough maturity to admit, as we reminisced about the trip, that, yes, I'd been spitefully moving forward, simply because I'd been *told* not to, rather than asked.

I was, at that time, approximately 54 years old. That is far too old to not be able to acknowledge a bit of spite.

LEARN TO HEAP BURNING COALS OF KINDNESS: Do this humbly, and with real love, so as not to manipulate someone with feelings of guilt, nor to take a spiteful glee in it. Above we read a bit from St. Paul's letter to the Romans, where he writes "if your enemy is hungry, feed him; if he is thirsty, give him something to drink; for by so doing you will heap burning coals upon his head."

In Rumer Godden's great novel *In This House of Brede*, a young nun, whose vocation had been challenged and denigrated by an older nun from the moment of her entrance until the day of her solemn vows, discovered that she was in the position to do something uniquely helpful to the older nun, and did it without giving it another thought. When the younger sister's kindness was discovered, the older nun went to their abbess, who was fully aware of the dynamic between them, and bowed her head in shame. "Hot coals," she said to the abbess, "and they burn." There was nothing for the abbess to say, beyond "I am sure they do."

Hot coals burn away the meanness of the other, and also your need to hold on to it. It is really just St. Paul speaking to us once again: "Do not be conquered by evil but conquer evil with good."

ASK OUR GUARDIAN ANGELS FOR AN ASSIST: They are messengers, but also warriors of a sort. They'll guide you in keeping things fair and ethical, especially when none of these suggestions seem natural to us.

PRAY
(THIS PRAYER OR YOUR OWN)

Lord, it seems like we are forever resisting the wiles of our own egos that urge us, out of the depths of our subconscious thinking, to make ourselves seen, known, and loved, by any means necessary, even if that means through the spiteful actions, malicious intentions, and passive bullying that cause injury and discord in the lives of others. We know that you reward meekness over aggression, but we are not always comfortable with that, largely because we are not even certain what meekness means, but none of us want to feel like a chump. We beg you to guide our thoughts and actions when we are in a place of emotional noise and inse-curity. When our inner voice is telling us to get back at someone for the sake of our dignity, remind us that nothing we can do will confer a greater dignity upon us than being obedient to your call to turn the other cheek, and to go the extra mile. In this way, we create space for mature and open reconciliation with our broth-ers and with heaven. We ask this faithfully, in the name of Christ Jesus. Amen.

CHAPTER NINE

Clinging to Our Narratives Beyond Their Usefulness

Attachment is the great fabricator of illusions; reality can be obtained only by someone who is detached.
— Simone Weil

Not long ago, I was talking to a very sweet, very devout young Catholic woman who shared her frustration as she discerns whether she is being called to some form of consecrated religious life. The message she kept getting, from various religious communities, was that she was probably unsuitable; one group told her not to even bother to visit on a "come and see" weekend (a kind of open house, where discerners get to see religious life up close and personal).

As you might imagine, that message was pretty hurtful; it left a mark.

I suspected the problem might lie in this young woman's habit of being way too quick to volunteer information about herself that would be better-shared after people had gotten to know her for the lovely, helpful, and undemanding person I have always found her to be, and not the high-maintenance penance she presents herself as when she introduces herself with "I have a learning disability and food allergies."

She is a Catholic girl, you understand, and sometimes it's difficult, particularly for those of us raised Catholic, to put our best foot forward without tripping over the big rock of humiliation we hurl around ourselves with every step of our bad foot. To introduce oneself with "Hi, I'm Mary, and I'm an accomplished grad student, inquiring about your religious community (or your job opening)" feels like blowing our horns too loudly; it feels unnatural, and while I can't speak for men, I know for many Catholic women it often seems like we're being not just immodest but — as my mother would say — "brassy and unladylike."

This is a real thing. I am by no means one of those people who go for cheap laughs by using tired "Catholic guilt" tropes. I actually do not believe that there is such a thing as "Catholic guilt," but there is such a thing as a Catholic conscience — a mind trained to recognize when our behavior is not just sinful (already a socially backward idea) but also just plain crass.

The inability to distinguish between "sinful and also crass" behavior and "truthful assertiveness" is where my young friend, like so many of us, does a crash-and-burn. Unwilling to introduce herself with anything hinting at head-on braggadocio, she would throw herself into reverse and then repeatedly smash into every house she liked with her trunkful of fine fragilities. Thus were her contacts, and her hopes, crushed before anyone could even see the beauty of the driver.

I understand, dear reader, that having spent a few chapters with me, you are sitting there guffawing, and wondering if I am so lacking in self-awareness that I cannot see myself in that description of my friend. Of course I can. I am quite certain I have never delivered a column or a manuscript to an editor without telling him or her, "I hope it's useful." When someone writes to tell me that they enjoyed my last books, *Strange Gods* or *I Don't Want to Be a Hoo-er*, my grateful reply usually starts with "I'm so thrilled when people don't think my stuff is utter garbage" — a sentiment that would seem to belie my ever writing a word intended for publication, and yet nevertheless reflects my true feelings.

It's not just me. I know perhaps a dozen Catholic writers — mostly women, but some men as well — who have produced multiple successful and well-regarded books, but suffered through the process of promoting their product; with asking people to review their work; with talking about themselves-and-the-book-and-the-book-and-themselves for the requisite month-to-six-weeks of pre-and-post-book launch. It should be fun and delightful — and parts of it are, of course — and yet part of it also feels so in-your-face and impolite!

I know it is a strictly cradle-Catholic problem, by the way, because my writer friends who were formerly atheists, or are up-from-Protestantism, have no such qualms: they manage to do their self-promotional duties with an impressive sense of excitement and casual aplomb, while we cradle Catholics push our books forward gingerly and say, "Um, I wrote this thing ... if you want to read it. I think it's not horrible. You won't die of the plague as you read it."

The point is this: every story has a narrative thrust, and so do the stories of our lives. We should certainly want to share them, particularly if, in the course of self-revelation, we can manage to be both interesting and also throw a little insight into the shared mysteries of life that give us the tumbles. But what stories we choose to share in building that narrative should never become so stuck to us that we are forever defined by them — and when we start out acting like life is a perpetual support group, introducing ourselves with our name and our issue, that's precisely what we do. I once got into an elevator with a woman, and before we'd reached the sixth floor she informed me she was in three different 12-Step groups.

That's an extreme example, and obviously that lady must have had a great deal weighing on her to have come at a perfect stranger with such a head-on declaration of her damage. Still, it's a thing that we do, in smaller ways, as we go about constructing the narrative arc of our stories. More often than not, it doesn't really work out well for us, even if we think we're being cute about it:

- "Hi, I'm Anna. I have six kids, a job, and a dog, and am so glad to be with the grown-ups tonight that I'm carrying two glasses of wine" is a funny and identifiable line that, used too often, can define you as overwhelmed and desperate.
- "Hi, I'm Deacon Joe, and I get to do all of these baptisms because the pastor likes golf" is also cute — until it begins to paint you as bitter.
- "Hi, I'm Elizabeth, and I don't just want a makeover; I want a half-century-long do-over" is a funny line that eventually will make everyone else want Anna's two drinks.

The habit of self-denigration in the name of humility is not really sinful in a usual way of thinking. Because it's usually employed as a safeguard against pride, it should actually be accounted a good habit, shouldn't it?

Well, no, not if we believe that we were loved into being and created in God's image:

"You are precious in my eyes." (Is 43:4, RSV)

Self-denigration stops being healthy and starts becoming sinful when it serves to create a despicable or pitiable narrative that we then cling to, and eventually allow to utterly ensnare us in characterizations that we can no longer control or amend.

The sin itself is partly one of a paradoxical pride ("Look how humble I am!"), but this is a twofold kind of fault, as there is also an element of narrowness to it that refuses to work with God — refuses to let our narratives grow, or our arcs widen, so that the Holy Spirit may have room to work.

I'm certainly as susceptible to this sin as anyone, but I have also gotten an assist in (slowly) working my way out of it, and from the unlikeliest of events: the Vatican's investigation into the Leadership Council of Women Religious, which recently concluded on a very good note for the Church, all around.

When the story first broke, I was praying about it, for the sake of the sisters and the Church, and wondering about the prevailing narrative: excellent sisters who have been a kind of Central Nervous System for the American Church (and practically the inventors of the idea of social-service networks), being harassed by the aloof and mean men of the Church.

I knew that *couldn't* be all to the narrative — and by the end, it was not — but in those first angry days, I wondered if an opening up of the prevailing story arc might help to effect reconciliation.

After all, it had worked for my mother and me.[12]

My mother — let's call her Alice, because she liked that name — was born during the Depression to a couple who could neither hear nor speak, and were rather famous around Coney Island for their ability to initiate spontaneous parties and sustain them for whole weekends.

They were the polar opposite of today's "helicopter parents." For them, parenting was not half as interesting as playing the ponies, their factory-shift work, or partying with their fellows (had the word "homies" then been in vogue, I have no doubt that Gran and Granpa would have used it, turned their caps backward, stuck out their tongues, and folded their arms with nods full of attitude), so they frequently left Alice under the long-term supervision of a rather bitter grandmother, who taught her how to sew, bake, and weed a garden with such resolute vigor that I never saw Alice do any of those things during my lifetime.

While Alice was faithfully, if rather sternly, clothed, fed, and taught her catechism by her grandmother, it was her glamorous-seeming parents who captured her imagination and on whom she modeled her own personality. As a mother, she, too, was dutiful — if the meals were awful, the school uniforms were pressed and the lunches made — but she parented with a determined eccentricity as well. Returning from school one day, my brother noted that most of his closet was strewn about the neighborhood, one shirt still dangling from his bedroom window. Laughing, he gathered up clothes as he walked, and explained, "Yeah, I forgot to make my bed this morning. She hates that."

Dutiful and a bit daft, my mother might be a prime example of how we are formed by our nature and our nurturers, but her decidedly non-hovering style helped her children to become self-sufficient as well; if she did not gush about our gifts or accomplishments — she was more inclined toward jeering — she was the first to say, "If you want to try it, you should. Go! Work hard! Send a postcard!"

Perhaps because her upbringing placed her between a boozy, cheerful but silent world and the grim-but-educated alternative, Alice adored multi-syllabic pronouncements: she memorized poems, speeches, and soliloquies. She gave to me a love of words — the ability to take joy from phrases tripping nimbly from the tongue, and in giddy, delight-laden alliterations. Not all of the memories are good ones, but drunk or sober, angry or gleeful, the stuff that poured from her mouth would routinely stop me in my tracks for the sheer glory of it all.

While she was still alive, and I had matured a bit, I wrote Alice a note, thanking her for her fine madness, for her willingness to give me my own head when I needed to go, and for all the words I'd received from her — the stupid ones, the slurred ones, the brilliant ones. "Without intention, without realizing it, you have handed me my profession on a platter," I wrote. "Amid all the coal mined in our time together, there have been these diamonds, and I will not forget."

Was our relationship made perfect by that? No. But my ability to see through a forest of anger to acknowledge the fruitful trees Alice had planted for my eventual gleaning was the beginning of a change in the narrative arc. I began to feel much less defined by the bitter memories of abuse, and able to look at both her life and my own with enough rueful humor and appreciation so as to develop real gratitude for her, and for everything — good times and bad. The thrust of my own narrative developed side stories of mercy and forgiveness — and even, yes, a little healthy pride.

So, when I prayed for the LCWR sisters and a peaceful resolution to their contretemps with Rome, I wondered if they were being underserved by the popular narrative, which indeed at the time they seemed to want to cling to, and whether they, too, needed to find a way to open their grasp just a little bit, for the sake of the Holy Spirit.

Would they be willing to look at their relationship with Rome as I had mine with Alice? Could they ever admit — as the media surely would not — that the imperfect, "dutiful and daft" Church hierarchs bothering them were also the ones who had been willing to give women their heads when no other institution and no "respectable" society in the world would; that when a woman said she was called by God to take in orphans, build a hospital, start a school, or go on a mission in the Congo, the men of the Church didn't condescendingly ask them instead to sew a quilt or growl, "Pipe down and make me a sandwich." What they said was, "If you want to try it, you should. Go! Work hard! Send a postcard!"

It is a small but very healing thing to look back, even in anger, and acknowledge where — amid all the coal — the pressure actually formed diamonds. It is how both the self-denigrating or prideful narratives to which we inordinately cling become open so that we may eventually detach from them, and reach out more fully to God.

—

WHAT DOES CATHOLICISM HAVE TO SAY ABOUT NARRATIVE DETACHMENT?

Give me ten truly detached men, and I will convert
the world with them.
— St. Philip Neri

When self-will and ease become habitual,
they overthrow a man.
— Abba Poemen

[Faith in one God] *means making good use of
created things*: faith in God, the only One, leads us
to use everything that is not God only insofar
as it brings us closer to him, and to detach ourselves
from it insofar as it turns us away from him:

My Lord and my God, take from me everything
that distances me from you. My Lord and my God, give me
everything that brings me closer to you. My Lord and my God,
detach me from myself to give my all to you.[13]
— Catechism of the Catholic Church
(n. 226, emphasis in original)

Let nothing trouble you,
Let nothing frighten you;
Everything passes;
God never changes;
Patience
Obtains all;
Whoever has God
Wants for nothing;
God alone is enough.
— St. Teresa of Ávila

This life is not everything. There is an eternity. Today, it is
very unmodern to say this, even in theology. To speak of life
beyond death looks like a flight from life here on earth. But what if it
is true? Can one simply pass it by? Can one dismiss it as
mere consolation? Is it not precisely this reality that bestows
on life its seriousness, its freedom, its hope?
— POPE BENEDICT XVI[14]

Perish every fond ambition,
All I've thought and hoped and known,
Yet how rich is my condition!
God and Heaven are still my own.
— HENRY LYTE

To be detached does not mean to be indifferent or uninterested.
It means to be nonpossessive. Life is a gift to be grateful for
and not a property to cling to.
— HENRI J. M. NOUWEN[15]

By and by, nor spare a sigh
Though worlds of wanwood leafmeal lie;
And yet you will weep and know why.
Now no matter, child, the name:
Sorrow's springs are the same.
— GERARD MANLEY HOPKINS, "SPRING AND FALL"

I beg of you, my Lord,
to remove anything which separates
me from you, and you from me.
Remove anything that makes me unworthy
of your sight, your control, your reprehension;
of your speech and conversation,
of your benevolence and love.
Cast from me every evil
that stands in the way of my seeing you,
hearing, tasting, savoring, and touching you;

fearing and being mindful of you;
knowing, trusting, loving, and possessing you;
being conscious of your presence
and, as far as may be, enjoying you.
This is what I ask for myself
and earnestly desire from you. Amen.
— St. Peter Faber

—

HOW DO WE BREAK THE HABIT OF
OVER-ATTACHMENT TO OUR NARRATIVES?

Detach: Breaking this habit is really hard. So hard, in fact, that I wonder if the best answer is simply to be *willing* to detach from our preferred narratives — our preferred way of thinking about and presenting ourselves to the world — in any given moment: to be *willing* to follow the curve of the Holy Spirit, particularly when interiorly we are squelching.

I have a friend who has taken up walking every morning, and after not seeing her for a few months, I couldn't help but comment on how well she looked; her eyes and skin were glowing, and she had lost weight. But her narrative was such that even though on some level she had to know she looked great, she simply couldn't bear to hear it, and quickly objected that, no, she looked awful and was gaining weight, not losing it, that week. Maybe a willingness to detach from a narrative is as simple as managing to smile and say "Thank you" when complimented; to resist the urge to automatically put oneself down.

Contrariwise, perhaps it is also to resist the urge to gloat about how great it's all going for you, if that's the direction toward which you are inclined, and simply acknowledge, "I'm very happy."

These are simple responses, and they suggest that the best way to detach from this really rather complex sin is to keep to simplicity. "Let your 'Yes' mean 'Yes,' and your 'No' mean 'No,' " said Christ Jesus. "Anything more is from the evil one" (Mt 5:37, NAB).

Yes, that pretty much sums it up, doesn't it? It is perfect instruction on detachment from narratives. Look at all the room it leaves for the Holy Spirit to work!

PRAY
(THIS PRAYER OR YOUR OWN)

Lord, I say too much. Too often my words and my presentment are wrung through with a need to protect myself, and how I wish to be seen — or not seen. My attempt to project a preferred narrative is based too much on trying to control what others think and say about me, or perhaps, what I want to think and say about myself. Clasping too hard to all of this keeps me a little edgy, and that keeps me from being truly open to you and your workings in my life. Guide me in the way of simple detachment from these concerns; let my "yes" be "yes," and my "no" be "no," in order to keep straight lines of clarity from becoming tangled and confused, to the benefit of everyone you bring before me. I ask this through Christ Jesus, your Son, who is the Way, the Truth, and the Light. Amen.

CHAPTER TEN

Half-Assing It, aka "Phoning It In"

Lisa, if you don't like your job, you don't strike. You just go in every day and do it really half-assed. That's the American way.

— Homer Simpson

Have you ever had the experience of meeting someone who works with a family member, and hearing what a productive, industrious, and conscientious co-worker he or she is? I recall picking my then-teenaged son up from work one day and having his boss stop to tell me what a terrific work ethic he had. "He really takes pride in his work and does a great job," the boss told me, as my son blushed scarlet.

I assured the supervisor that I was pleased to hear it, and as we drove away I began to bust my son's chops.

"Pride in your work and super-conscientious, are you? Then how come when you 'clean up' a blob of jelly in our kitchen, you do it so half-assed that the ants start lining up two blocks over?"

"It's different," my son laughed. "You're not paying me."

"Nor would I ever," I said.

The truth is, had I paid my son to clean his room and the kitchen table, he would have still done a lousy job of it, or — more likely — he wouldn't have done it at all, telling me to keep my money. When it comes to home and family, it's rare that any of us put as much effort into what's before us as we do at work.

And that is perhaps understandable. At work — particularly if we like our job — we have ambitions and ends that must be met. We comport ourselves appropriately and then work to achieve our goals. We put our best effort forward, and also expend the best of our energy.

At home? Groucho Marx said, "Home is where you hang your head," and even if that's not always true — or ever — it's true that home is where we can do our "second-best." At home, we ignore people or roll our eyes in ways we never can at work. At home, we dress down, scratch what itches, goof and tease, and even leave the beds unmade once in a while, because we know we can. We trust that a poorly wiped blob of grape jelly does not stain our chances for advancement — and if we put aside the mop in mid swab in order to graze a catalog that has caught our eye, who is to say we shouldn't?

Still, there is a difference between getting our chores done at our leisure — which doesn't especially mean doing it poorly — and actually half-assing the work before us, where we sort of put in an appearance, or "phone it in" altogether.

When my elder son, who talked early and often, was about five years old, he discovered video games, and if we went to the mall he'd always ask if we could spend some quarters at the arcade, and I'd always say yes — but seriously, nothing was more boring to me. I stood beside him as he played — mostly because I was obsessed with keeping him near me for his safety — and he would talk and talk and talk about whatever game he was playing, and I would basically say "Oh, really?" and "Mmm-hmm" and "Wow," with my eyes glazing over, until the quarters ran out.

I mean, he enjoyed the games, but I was half-assing my motherhood the entire time, and I'm pretty sure he knew it. I was "phoning in" my attention.

I confess that while I have always given 100 percent to my professional projects, I've phoned in way too much of my private life, and it shows. I start a diet plan and give it 100 percent for the first two weeks, perhaps 80 percent the week after that, 40 percent the next month — and before you know it, yeah, that's over. I start crocheting something, and three weeks later it gets shoved into a closet. I sweep the porch but don't move the chairs to really be thorough. I don't put the aspirin back where it belongs, and then when my husband needs it I roll my eyes as I go track it down for him. I forget half the things I go to the store for, I'm late with thank-you notes, and I have been known to hand-wash the dishes from lunch rather than empty the dishwasher.

All of my personal chores and commitments are first-world chores and commitments — which means they are not particularly taxing; I'm not carrying 20 gallons of water home for the day's washing — yet I half-ass them, all the time.

The truth is, none of the chores unconnected to work seem that important or pressing to me. Nothing is urgent. Everything will get done when it gets done — and even if I do a so-so job of it, who cares, really? Does it matter?

Well, it should matter to me because I am a Benedictine Oblate, and monastic Benedictines will tell you that thoroughness is a hallmark of the Holy Rule of St. Benedict: you scrub the pan thoroughly; you leave nothing lie; when you close the window, you lock it; when you put away the broom, you put it away; you don't just launch it somewhere into the garage.

It is about maturity and mindfulness, about seeing everything in its completeness and pursuing completeness in your craft — and your craft is whatever is before you. Laziness and inattention to our responsibilities speaks to sloth, and also to plain old selfishness.

These lessons have taken hold in my life only very slowly because, as I have admitted many times, I am not an exemplary Benedictine. Were I in a monastic community, I'd be the sister continually kissing the very floor I'd washed so poorly.

Ah, well, as Michelangelo is purported to have said, "*Ancora imparo*" ("I am still learning"). I am not the Michelangelo of any part of my life, but as a Benedictine I am meant to aspire to mas-

tery of the task before me — whether it is housework, or mother-
ing, or loving my neighbor, or feeding my husband, or putting the
aspirin back where it belongs — for the sake of my family and my
surroundings, and for the glory of God. St. Benedict wrote of the
necessity of "holy leisure" and the need for refreshment, but that
was meant to come after all our work is done, not before it and
certainly not — as sometimes happens in my world — right in
the middle of the job. *Ancora imparo, perdonami.*

Recently, I was reminiscing with my husband about our elder
son and how he had resented homework more than any child we'd
ever known. His philosophy, even in elementary school, was that
he had put his time in (in *the classroom*), and that school had no
business infringing upon his "own time" — which was meant for
himself, his own imaginings and interests — and because that was
true, he would rush through his homework, cutting corners, not
caring if it was neat or complete. He would half-ass the homework because, in his mind, that's all it was due.

It's an amusing memory, but one that got me to wondering
whether all of us are feeling so intruded upon in our lives (the Internet and our iPhones and the interconnectedness of everything
mean we are constantly pulled at, and rarely simply quiet and
recollected) that we have become desperate to enjoy a little of our
"own time," and in pursuit of it we are half-assing things — important things in our lives — and are no longer even aware of it.

My younger son recently recounted a scene at a fast-food
place that had upset him. A mother and her son — who looked
to be about four years old — were having lunch, and while the
boy chattered and played with his food, his mother made those
"mmm-hmm" sounds and stared continually at her smart phone,
reading and texting.

"The little boy kept talking, trying to get his mother's attention, and she never looked up. She was just completely engrossed
in her phone. Finally, the kid got on his knees before her, took
her face in his hands and forced her head up so she would look

at him," my son said. "And when he did, the mom just said, 'Cut it out,' and pushed him aside and went back to her phone." The mother had not been rough in her actions, but the little boy just looked down afterward and stopped chattering.

I'm sure that the mother didn't mean to communicate to her son that he was unimportant to her, any more than I did when I would "mmm-hmm" my way through the video arcades with my older son, but that's how we half-ass parenthood. That's how we phone it in so that it doesn't intrude upon the thing we would rather be doing: our "own time."

So, sloth can be physical or spiritual; it can reside in self-ishness or inattentiveness. The Greek word for it is "acedia" — ἀκηδία, *akedia* — which translates as indifference or, more liter-ally, as "without care." It covers all manners of negligence, sadness, or idleness. Monastics since John Cassian have called acedia "the noonday demon," making note of how precisely it seems to dis-rupt what we might call the "peak" of every day — the time when we should perhaps be most on our game.

I have a theory that the reason so many of us are looking to find a bit of our "own time," and therefore half-assing it, is not only because of the noise and intrusiveness of the world, but because a great number of us — perhaps a majority of us — are wandering around suffering from jumbo-sized, entrenched cases of acedia, and we don't even know it.

Here is how I described acedia, once, on my blog:

> For whatever reason, I have most uncharacteristically been doing battle, all week, with the devilish little blue megrim that is acedia.

> Actually, "doing battle" sounds romantic and pro-active. It would be more accurate to say I have been whining and unable to work, and whining about being unable to work, and wandering around the house ineffectually, and walking

the park feeding ducks, and missing my dog, and cooking supper and sitting before my oratory with nothing but a keening emptiness in my heart and mind and soul.

It is terrible to realize that you're a walking, aching void. Acedia is like a dark echo chamber of "me" bouncing off walls and resounding until nothing can get through the thickness of the self.

When you feel like that, it's very difficult to be thorough anywhere; phoning it in feels like a full measure of effort. It feels like all you can bear to do.

If I am right, and much of society is wandering about suffering from a case of spiritual acedia, all unawares, it may make our neglectfulness seem less sinful than pathetic and pitiably ill, but we shouldn't take consolation in it. Intentional or not, acedia still slips in on a spirit of sloth. It still needs to be addressed, and not made welcome. Evagrius of Pontus calls acedia "the most troubling of all" of the "eight bad thoughts" — though it somehow didn't make it into the eventual list of seven deadly sins — because it ensnares us in a constant twilight that can only lead to full-on spiritual darkness.

Think about it the next time you're "mmm-hmming" someone, not fully attending to the person before you, or claiming that a diminished attention span has kept you from doing the job that has been placed before you, and no one else.

—

WHAT DOES CATHOLICISM SAY ABOUT "PHONING IT IN," INATTENTIVENESS AND SLOTH, OR ACEDIA?

If the work of our sanctification presents, apparently, the most insurmountable difficulties, it is because we do not know how to form a just idea of it. In reality sanctity can be reduced to one single

practice, fidelity to the duties appointed by God.
Now this fidelity is equally within each one's power
whether in its active practice, or passive exercise.
The active practice of fidelity consists in accomplishing
the duties which devolve upon us whether imposed by the
general laws of God and of the Church, or by the
particular state that we may have embraced.
Its passive exercise consists in the loving acceptance
of all that God sends us at each moment.
— Jean-Pierre de Caussade, *Abandonment to Divine Providence*

It is easier to mend neglect than to quicken love.
— St. Jerome

You drag along like a bag of sand. You don't do your share.
And so it's not strange that you are beginning to feel the
first symptoms of lukewarmness. Wake up!
— St. Josemaría Escrivá

Acedia or spiritual sloth goes so far as to refuse the joy that comes
from God, and to be repelled by divine goodness.
— Catechism of the Catholic Church (n. 2094)

Only humility is victorious over this sin [acedia].
— Amma Theodora

Since sloth is a very deep drive, we must cast ourselves on the care
of God with great humility, recognizing our poverty and seeking his
miraculous grace to give us grateful, loving and passionate hearts.
— Monsignor Charles Pope

The true servant of Jesus Christ bears all things; she labors much,
and speaks little.
— St. Mary Magdalene de' Pazzi

—

HOW DO WE BREAK THE HABIT OF
HALF-ASSING IT; HOW DO WE DEFEAT ACEDIA?

DO GOD'S WORK: In Rumer Godden's *In This House of Brede*, a nun, whose talent as a sculptress has become renowned in art circles well beyond the enclosure of her abbey, is elected abbess. A friend and art critic writes to her, "This is absurd. When will you have time for your own work?"

"I have no 'own work,' " the new abbess responded. "I do God's work."

Perhaps on my twentieth reading of the book, I suddenly understood the depths of what the newly elected Abbess Hester Cunningham Proctor was relating to her friend, and it is precisely the mind-set we must adopt if we wish to stop phoning it in and half-assing our way through our lives. Consider the work before you — whether it be dusting, parenting, reading a report, changing a diaper, driving in traffic, visiting an older relative, volunteering, taking out the trash — and then consider that you really do not have any work of your own; *all of the world before you is "God's work,"* the task which has been assigned to you in that particular moment.

If we are doing God's work, we cannot afford to phone it in; you don't have the luxury of making a half-assed job of it. We will be graded on it. Like punctuation and penmanship, it will count.

PRAY THE PSALMS: To combat acedia, St. Teresa of Ávila offered a one-word prescription: *psalmody, psalmody, psalmody!* I have frankly found the prescription works, especially after taking a little advice from St. Benedict, who tells us to bring acedia (or any "bad thought") to the cross and "dash it against the rock of Christ." Dashing oneself against the cross, and then applying the psalms: it is the recipe, the chemistry, the holy prescription. I have known it for years, and yet when acedia snags me, it takes days to remember it. Still, it always works. In the psalmody, I find my own stubborn recalcitrance, born in the idolatry of my own service to my woes and feelings — and God's ever-willingness to deal with me:

> A voice I did not know said to me:
> "I freed your shoulder from the burden;
> your hands were freed from the load.
> You called in distress and I saved you.
>
> I answered, concealed in the storm cloud;
> at the waters of Meribah I tested you.
> Listen, my people, to my warning.
> O Israel, if only you would heed!
>
> Let there be no foreign god among you.
> no worship of an alien god.
> I am the Lord your God,
> who brought you from the land of Egypt.
> Open wide your mouth and I will fill it." (Ps 81:6b-10)

In psalmody, we remain nearer to the light than the shadows.

MAKE A DAILY SACRIFICE: "Reformation should begin with some small sacrifices. But be faithful and consistent in their performance. Don't bite off too much at once. Just as exercise restores a lost muscle tone, a daily sacrifice will restore spiritual vigor and vitality. It will increase your joy in living too" (Father Kilian Mc-Gowan, C.P.).

PRAY

(THIS PRAYER OR YOUR OWN)

O God, you know all things before we bring them to you, and yet often we do not even know our own minds or understand our moods, and in that case our prayer is always incomplete and must be supplemented by the intercession of the Holy Spirit. When our lives seem out of our own control, and fully under the power of indifference, sloth, acedia, and a sense of disengaged inattention, help us to recognize it quickly and bring our need to you in all humility. Help us to see our neediness as a grace, because within it we are so utterly dependent upon your merciful goodness, for we know that what you want for us is our freedom from such ineffable darkness, that we might live in your marvelous light. We ask this through your Son, our Lord, Christ Jesus. Amen.

CHAPTER ELEVEN

Cheating

The first and worst of all frauds is to cheat one's self.
All sin is easy after that.
— Pearl Bailey, attributed

The memory still stings: there I was, age 7, the veteran of a splendidly moving and memorable first holy Communion, and graced with an oddball love of the Sacrament of Confession in all of its velvet-curtained-sliding-screen ambiance, planning to steal a toy "ladies fan" from a candy store, simply to see if I could.

The fan was red, and I had always been — and still am — a sucker for all things red. It was airy, lacy, and flamboyant, and I had the 10 cents the thing cost in my pocket.

But the toy display was on the other side of the cashier, and the devil was on my shoulder: "Take it," he whispered. "I bet you could slip it into your pocket, and no one would know."

Petty theft, which I had never before aspired to, became suddenly a tantalizing challenge. And the fan was red. I took it. I cleverly slipped the thing into my sleeve and casually walked out the door. It was so easy. And so completely unsatisfying.

By the time I'd walked home, fanning myself all the way in a manner I was sure duplicated the graceful lines of a *señorita*, I had begun to feel a peculiar emptiness that was new, and throughout the day that feeling grew, until it threatened to become a black hole into which I could disappear. By eventide, I had thrown the fan away from me in disgust. It wasn't mine; it was ill-gotten booty. I had sinned, and it was not good.

The next day was Saturday — confession day in our neighborhood, for in 1965 it was a rare Catholic who would receive Communion without first reconciling themselves to God. I frankly couldn't wait to get the theft off my chest — and out of my heart and soul — and had barely gotten the "Bless me, Father" off my tongue before the full story came pouring out. The priest, spending another glorious Saturday within a small, airless box and — at that hour — listening mostly to the piping sins of children, had given a grumpy acknowledgement that my sin was a biggie. "Stealing is mentioned in the Ten Commandments; it especially offends God," he said, and I thought, "I know, I know. It's been eating at me."

Thank God for penance. A Rosary decade on my knees felt sufficiently arduous, and I emerged from church feeling like I'd done my piece. And yet ... it couldn't be that easy, could it? Where was the justice? The man at the candy store was still out his 10 cents.

Walking home, I fingered the quarter in my pocket, given to me by my grandmother and designated for an orange drink I craved. My sense of justice wrestled with my thirst. I did dearly love my orange drink. But finally, conscience won out. Stepping into the candy store, I approached the counter, meaning to confess my crime, pay the dime, and be done. But I couldn't. Serving justice on a coward's tray, I waited until the man's attention was diverted, and quietly slid the quarter on his counter and quickly left the store.

It was not a perfectly balanced redemption: it left me cleansed, but out 15 cents. But I had not yet explored the vagaries of fairness. I was ignorant of all but the most elementary theology, and it would be many years before I could distinguish between the unsophisticated notion of "Catholic guilt" and the heavy grace of what Father Joseph Parisi calls "a properly formed conscience," but I felt better. My Catholic grounding had informed my sense of both justice and mercy. I had confessed regret to my God and made a generous, if anonymous, restitution, and the gaping mouth of emptiness so eager to swallow me had been resolutely snapped shut. The red fan was never again a pleasurable toy, but it became a favorite possession, a reminder that whenever God is pushed aside, only emptiness awaits.[16]

That's most of a piece I wrote in 2012, for *The Catholic Answer* magazine — a friend calls it my "Augustine and the pears" story — and I reproduce it here, not to cheat my way through this chapter, as some might suspect, but because it is so appropriate to the topic, particularly the fallout that occurred from these six words: *simply to see if I could.*

I think most people, unless they are burdened with a character defect or a deep psychological problem, tend to be honest, and to think of themselves as honest — I know I do, or did, until I started ruminating on this chapter — but we also have something in us that thinks if we can "get away" with a thing, usually a small thing, then that's perfectly fine:

- I can take a few sleeves of staples from work to home. It's fine. It's like 80 staples, who cares?
- As long as I get the job done, I can use some of my time at work to read blogs and play on Facebook; everyone does that.
- I can eat this ice cream, and no one will know that I've cheated on my diet.
- I can pad the expense account with a couple of "under 10 dollars, so no receipt needed" items each month. So what? It's a couple of hundred a year, maybe. This place has sucked at least that much extra time from me.

Imagine that one person has said all of these things, and you get an idea of how a dubious action, rationalized away, begets another, slightly bigger one, and then another slightly bigger one than that. A small cheat here and there, too small to really be noticed, and suddenly we are not only rationalizing our behavior, but we're developing a sense of entitlement as well.

As I write this, I am reading about a debate taking place in New York City, as to whether turnstile jumping — that is, not paying the fare in order to ride the subway — should be overlooked by the transit police. Some youngsters, it seems (or oldsters, if they are fit enough to jump), should not be taken to task for stealing a ride they may not otherwise be able to afford. In response, some are calling this an imperfect, and immoral, solution, and I may agree. By all means, if someone cannot afford the ever-increasing fares, let the city find a way to subsidize people who need help. But simply making an exception for some of our more bold and limber citizens, while expecting others — many of whom may be heading to work, with a dollar and a subway token in the pocket, as I once did — to pony up their fair share, simply because they're too old for hurdling? It strikes some people as a poorly thought-out solution; it strikes others as an entitled exception for cheating.

That can't be good. No one is ever entitled to cheat, whether in goods, or at a board game, or on taxes. But the mind-set that we're entitled to "get away" with a little something exists, even among we who think of ourselves as honest.

About 30 years ago, a friend, who has a bit of a mischievous streak in her, visited a garden store with me and tried slipping a tiny cactus into a small basket. "I bet if I brought these together at the register, they'd just charge me for the basket," she laughed.

The horrors of my childhood fan-theft came rushing to the fore of my memory, and I gasped. "That would be stealing!" I said.

She sighed and then grumbled, "It's not like I'm a thief and I'm robbing a bank," and she separated the plant from the basket. When we checked out, she made a point of showing me that she'd kept them apart, but as we walked to the car she groused at me, asking, "When did you become such a fuddy-duddy, anyway?"

"When I was 7," I said.

"Horrible child," she declared. "I wouldn't have played with you!"

I said I had considered myself to be an essentially honest person, prior to mapping out this chapter, and I think that's mostly true, but I also know that I do plenty of "cheating" things in the course of a day. Some of it falls under the category of "half-assing it," as discussed in the previous chapter. As we see repeatedly throughout this book, our little bad habits are multilayered, interconnected little sins, so quick to lead us from the grass into the weeds, and from the weeds into the swamplands.

Because that's true, some of my cheating takes the form of the "little sin" of procrastination, which we discussed much earlier. Before I typed up this chapter, for instance, I spent more time than I should have online, looking at the history of tiaras. I'm not particularly interested in tiaras, but if I'm procrastinating about writing, I'd rather read about tiaras than wash the kitchen floor. Which means I not only cheated my editor of an on-time chapter, but I cheated the household too, because the floor could stand a good mopping, and when the family troops in tonight, I'll probably say something like, "I meant to wash the floor today, but I got so busy!"

Which would be a lie. Because even though I have finally gotten busy typing this chapter, I never had any intention of washing the floor. I meant to not wash it.

So the procrastination on typing up a chapter on cheating will lead me to cheating and lying. I've just made my own point for myself!

Of course, I could type the chapter and simply not mention the dirty floor to my family, because they basically won't notice, anyway. But then I'll be holding a secret, and secret keeping is another kind of cheating.

Not all secrets are cheats, of course. Some secrets are delightful, and meant for eventual exposure. Some secrets — if they are not criminal or colluding on something immoral — are better kept to oneself, lest one needlessly burden another. Our sins and our dirty laundries, for instance, are kept between us and our priest, and whomever we have made reparation to, but they are no one else's business, so they are secrets best kept.

But secrets become a form of cheating when they redound to ourselves — our peace of mind, our self-esteem, or our own health and safety. I'm not much of a sneak-eater, except when I am trying hard to diet; then it is not unusual for me to snag a few cookies or a slice of forbidden bread — or a Homer Simpsonian *"forbidden donut"* — and keep it to myself — both literally and figuratively. But then I feel terrible about the sneak, so my conscience becomes as heavy as my thighs, and my sense of myself as a person of integrity goes by the wayside. I can't ignore having cheated myself, because when I get on the scale at the end of the week, the number hasn't moved. Or worse, it has moved in the wrong direction. Then the cheat — the undiscovered lie to myself, and anyone who has supported me in my latest dieting debacle — becomes obvious and exposed.

The sociologist and writer Cheryl Hughes has said, "When people cheat in any arena, they diminish themselves — they threaten their own self-esteem and their relationships with others by undermining the trust they have in their ability to succeed and in their ability to be true." That's true in every circumstance, whether we are cheating ourselves, cheating a store, cheating an employer (yes, reading blogs or posting pictures of your lunch to Facebook on company time really is cheating; it's a theft of time), cheating on a test for school, or cheating on a line or two of our tax return.

The "little sin" of "small cheats" speaks to greed, and to pride, and sometimes to lust. It may be a component of envy or gluttony — so yes, little cheats are big deals.

Our cheating always affects another, and it always hurts ourselves — and the truth is, there is no "getting away" with anything, because God sees it all, knows the content of our hearts, and understands our entire intention better (and before) we do.

One thing we are not thinking, when we're planning a little cheat and seeing what we can get away with: we don't think we're pulling a fast one on God. Such a thought would involve actually bringing God to mind, which would probably upset our game. When we cheat, we're not thinking of God at all.

Another excellent reason not to do it.

—

WHAT DOES CATHOLICISM SAY ABOUT SMALL CHEATS AND THEFTS?

"The person who is trustworthy in very small matters is also trustworthy in great ones; and the person who is dishonest in very small matters is also dishonest in great ones."
— Luke 16:10 (NAB)

Better to be poor and walk in integrity
than rich and crooked in one's ways.
— Proverbs 19:1 (NAB)

If we live good lives, the times are also good.
As we are, such are the times.
— St. Augustine

All have sinned and are deprived of the glory of God.
— Romans 3:23 (NAB)

Even if it does not contradict the provisions of civil law, any form of unjustly taking and keeping the property of others is against the seventh commandment: thus, deliberate retention of goods lent or of objects lost; business fraud; paying unjust wages; forcing up prices by taking advantage of the ignorance or hardship of another.[17]
— Catechism of the Catholic Church (n. 2409)

—

HOW DO WE AVOID FALLING INTO SUCH
A LITTLE AND COMMON SIN,
WHICH CAN BRING US SO LOW?

BE RUTHLESSLY HONEST — WITH YOURSELF: Let's face it, chopping off our hands, plucking out our eyes, or doing damage to our rationalization-happy brains are impractical solutions to, well, anything. What a propensity for cheating demands of us is a commitment to ruthless honesty.

We live in an age that does not appreciate such a thing: to be brutally honest with another is often considered rude and nearly always considered "insensitive" because it hurts. To be brutally honest with the self hurts too — it clarifies what is lacking in our own character — but it is also a dicey proposition. Once we are willing to admit to ourselves that we're not quite as honest as we think we are — and that if we think we can get away with something, we will probably try it — then we have to make sure we don't overcorrect ourselves into neurotic scrupulosity. We also have to remember that God is merciful, and that could tempt us into applying great dollops of mercy all over ourselves, which would, by doing nothing to change our behavior, probably sink us even further down into the pit.

What is necessary against this sin is sacramental confession: a real examination of where we have cheated, how we have done it, and what we thought we were getting out of it needs to be undertaken, and then confessed. Consider actually writing things down so that you can really be thorough in your admissions, because you are admitting things to God and to yourself, and naming one's sin aloud is often the catalyst for defeating it.

SEEK SPIRITUAL GUIDANCE: Consider finding a spiritual director. This is advice I have undertaken myself; because of all of my "little sins," it was my cheatin' heart that made me weep, and also made me realize that I needed someone to go to who could call me out about my behavior without making me feel unloved, defensive, or rejected, which is always how I react when my family does it. A good spiritual director can keep you from overindulging in your own personal penitential instincts, and also from allowing you to saturate yourself with mercy, when that's God's job. He or she will keep you humble, and it is humility, more than anything, that can beat back a strain of habitual dishonesty and help set you on a straighter, and free-er, path.

LISTEN TO YOUR GUARDIAN ANGEL: Finally, I know I have several times recommended invoking our guardian angels to help us to break these habits. It seems to me that on this issue of cheating — wherein so much of what is bad for us gets quickly and quietly rationalized away, all interiorly — we need someone there to talk us out of ourselves, to warn us away from our own sneaky voice. In this case, we need the whispers of the angels; we need their protection and their counsel.

So, every day, particularly as you approach the things that you now realize spark your cheating engine, ask your guardian angel to stand between you and that temptation, and to assist you with angelic strength.

This is downright saintly advice:

Make yourself familiar with the angels, and behold them frequently in spirit. Without being seen, they are present with you. (St. Francis de Sales)

When tempted, invoke your angel. He is more eager to help you than you are to be helped! Ignore the devil and do not be afraid of him: he trembles and flees at the sight of your guardian angel. (St. John Bosco)

Pray
(this prayer or your own)

There is no prayer I can make that speaks to this issue better than
Psalm 139, offered in true humility and repentance:

O Lord, you search me and you know me,
you know my resting and my rising,
you discern my purpose from afar.
You mark when I walk or lie down,
all my ways lie open to you.

Before ever a word is on my tongue
you know it, O Lord, through and through.
Behind and before you besiege me,
your hand ever laid upon me.
Too wonderful for me this knowledge,
too high, beyond my reach.

O where can I go from your spirit,
or where can I flee from your face?
If I climb the heavens, you are there.
If I lie in the grave, you are there.

If I take the wings of the dawn
and dwell at the sea's furthest end,
even there your hand would lead me,
your right hand would hold me fast.

If I say: "Let the darkness hide me
and the light around me be night,"
even darkness is not dark for you
and the night is as clear as the day
For it was you who created my being,

knit me together in my mother's womb.
I thank you for the wonder of my being,
for the wonders of all your creation.

Already you knew my soul,
my body held no secret from you
when I was being fashioned in secret
and molded in the depths of the earth.

Your eyes saw all my actions,
they were all of them written in your book;
every one of my days was decreed
before one of them came into being.

To me, how mysterious your thoughts,
the sum of them not to be numbered!
If I count them, they are more than the sand;
to finish, I must be eternal, like you.

O God, that you would slay the wicked!
Men of blood, keep far away from me!
With deceit they rebel against you
and set your designs at naught.

Do I not hate those who hate you,
abhor those who rise against you?
I hate them with a perfect hate
and they are foes to me.

O search me, God, and know my heart.
O test me and know my thoughts.
See that I follow not the wrong path
and lead me in the path of life eternal.

Chapter Twelve

Sins of Omission

I never cut my neighbor's throat;
My neighbor's gold I never stole;
I never spoiled his house and land;
But God have mercy on my soul!

For I am haunted night and day
By all the deeds I have not done;
O unattempted loveliness!
O costly valor never won!
— Marguerite Wilkinson

A curious thing about the *Novus Ordo* liturgy, at least as it is practiced in the United States, is that much of the Mass makes a point of emphasizing the horizontal — the outreach to the assembly and its responses — over the vertical, which involves our reach out to heaven and heaven's response to us. A perfect equilibrium of horizontal and vertical within the liturgy is a kind of conformity with the cross, by which Christ raised everything and everyone up from the dregs and effected a consummation of perfect reconciliation. As Chesterton noted, the cross — reaching North, South, East, and West — is all-encompassing, and that's rather wonderful to ponder as we consider our faith, and how we live it. Are we living our faith in an open and all-encompassing way that reflects the range and reach of the cross? Or are we rather self-enclosed, and contained, spinning in our own comfortable spheres?

As we have taken the circle as the symbol of [physicalist] reason and madness, we may very well take the cross as the symbol at once of mystery and health.... For the circle is perfect and infinite in nature; but it is fixed forever in its size; it can never be larger or smaller. But the cross, though it has at its heart a collision and a contradiction, can extend its four arms for ever without altering its shape. Because it has a paradox in its centre it can grow without changing. The circle returns upon itself and is bound. The cross opens its arms to the four winds; it is a signpost for free travellers. (G. K. Chesterton, *Orthodoxy*)

There is something to recommend bringing the horizontal and the vertical of the cross into our worship, into our lives, and even into our processes, but there must also be balance. Too much emphasis on the horizontal and the worship becomes mundane and then moribund; too much emphasis on the vertical, and it all gets so exalted and mystical that not the tiniest part of it seems relatable. Either way, our relationship to God — and our ability to function in the day-to-day of life — is negatively impacted.

Very often at Mass, as we approach the penitential rite, the echo chambers of my mind immediately fill my head with the sound of countless priests intoning the Confiteor. "I confess," the celebrant begins, and we all, as a community, join in:

... to almighty God,
and to you, my brothers and sisters,
that I have greatly sinned,
in my thoughts and in my words,
in what I have done and in what I have failed to do,
through my fault, through my fault,
through my most grievous fault;
therefore I ask blessed Mary ever-Virgin,

all the Angels and Saints,
and you, my brothers and sisters,
to pray for me to the Lord our God.

Even before this prayer was *fully* restored (post-Vatican II, the English translation had omitted the breast-beating self-accusation of distinctly personal *and grievous* fault), I had loved it because it is so perfectly vertical and horizontal; it reaches out to God and to the community and brings us all together in acknowledgement of sin, and includes heaven and earth, God and humanity, in the action of mercy.

Frankly, I love this prayer and always pray it with my whole heart, because when you proclaim it with your mouth and mind you are making a public declaration about yourself that is utterly true. Standing amidst your fellows, you admit, "I blew it. I am all that is human and fallible, and I have failed you. I have failed myself. I have failed heaven. Please pray for me."

The prayer is a confession — as a penitential rite within the Mass, it wipes away our venial sins — but it's also a great leveler. There may be an 80-year-old in the pew before you, saying the words, and an 8-year-old behind you, beating his breast, but the three of you (and everyone else in church) are standing in solidarity, recognizing that we're all in the same boat, that we've all, since our last assembly, done what humans do: we've screwed up.

We see, too, that our actions do not happen in a vacuum, that when we do screw up out of selfishness, or self-interestedness, we affect the larger society in ways small and large. Hopefully, we realize that it's beyond stupid to sit in judgment of one's neighbor's splinters when one is walking around like a right porcupine, oneself.

This is why the self-accusation of personal grievous fault needed to be restored to the prayer. It not only united us in prayer to the rest of the Catholic world (non-English translations had always retained it), but it also put the fault precisely where it belongs: on us.

There is something ironic about the fact that as the *Novus Ordo* brought more emphasis to the horizontal — brought so much more attention to us, to "we the people who are Church" — it simultaneously lost the emphasis on personal responsibility. The intention, I believe, was to de-emphasize the individual and encourage the formation of a holistic, human communion of worship, and that's not an awful aim.

But the truth is, in the end, we each go to God as a singularity. No matter how much we might promote community and like creating and participating in an organism of worship, we go to God alone, and before God we answer for our own behavior, not for the actions of our neighbor.

So that *mea culpa* — "through my fault, through my fault, through my most grievous fault" — is a dose of necessary humility and truth within a prayer of powerful purpose.

Some people don't like the *mea culpa*; they consider it a brusque negative, bruising to the psyche and hurtful.

Well, yes. Acknowledging that I, and no one else, am responsible for my sins is not especially pleasant. It is a hot poker to our illusions that we're all doing "fine."

And, too, it is uncomfortable to be vulnerable, and with the Confiteor, we make ourselves a bit naked before many who are strangers. But vulnerability is often the crack by which grace can enter in:

I have greatly sinned,
in my thoughts and in my words,
in what I have done, *and in what I have failed to do*
[emphasis added].

Who can't identify with that? Who can't look back on a week and not shake their heads in self-disappointment, at least at *some* of what one has done? And yet we come to Mass, to the Word, to prayer, to Communion, and we stand together, and we confess our commonality. We are more alike than we sometimes want to admit.

Like the Hosanna — which unites us to the prayer of the angels before the Holy Throne — the painful Confiteor is too beautiful, and too powerfully unitive a prayer, to be mumbled through.

I've spent this time examining the prayer because it's something I've thought a lot about. I have had to, because my sins of omission contain, amid the small ones (many of which are accounted in this book, as we've talked about phoning things in or overindulging the self), larger ones that have lately come back to haunt me. These are sins of omission that have involved really offering a part of our lives to some whose lives I believe my husband and I could truly have helped, had I only been willing to take on the difficult people who would have become part and parcel of the mission.

I'm thinking of three children (perhaps four) in particular, whose parents were so neglectful (or so challenged themselves) that, had my husband and I offered to take in the kids (not that it would have ever been as easy as that), these children might have had a better start in life.

They have become my sins of omission. They are all adults now, and I have no idea where any of them may be. But I pray for them often, through time and through space, and beg mercy for all I did not do for them.

The sin of omission wasn't my husband's; he is a sucker for kids and would have agreed to my ideas without hesitation. It was mine; the sin is all mine. My husband would have simply moved forward with trust, and probably built a dormer on the house.

I held back out of fear. I knew the parents well enough to know that taking on the children meant dealing with maddening, obnoxious, substance-addled, and just plain strange perpetual adolescents for years, and my own selfishness, my own obnoxious adolescence, couldn't get past those thoughts, couldn't simply trust. My instincts — perhaps by the prompting of the Holy Spirit — said, "These are great kids; reach out for them." But I did not.

My self-protectiveness was partly born of fear, and my fear was born of — you guessed it — the taint of deadly sins: my pride, my greed, and my sloth, made me unwilling. My pride kept me disinterested in dealing with these parents. My greed was for my own children, and my (really stupid, in hindsight) worries that bringing in more kids might mean less of me available for them. My sloth, well . . . my husband was traveling a great deal at that point, often for weeks at a time; the extra work would have been all on me, and I was unwilling. Stupid, stupid. Yes, I regret not trying.

To be fair to myself — because as you might have realized by now, I can *mea-culpa* and breast-beat with the best (or worst) of them, but even I know that personal circumstances do come into play — all of this was going on while I was also recovering from a medical issue that had precipitated some severe neurological damage; often my physical energy was less than optimal, my short-term memory was barely there, and my mental fog was formidable.

As a woman trained in counseling once told me (after I'd blurted all of this out to her over wine), had I actually made the effort, there was no guarantee that anything would have come from it beyond (perhaps) local social services becoming involved — and for all I knew, they already were.

Further, the fact that I'd be (essentially) single-parenting it while cognitively unwell might have precluded my ever being approved to foster anyone. My efforts could have, ironically, ended up with Child Protective Services opening a file on me, because some days it was all I could do to get off the couch and accomplish minimal parenting and housework myself.

I hadn't thought of that. She might well be correct. That doesn't negate the sin of omission, though, and this is why: as with all sin, intention matters. I saw a need and — regardless of circumstances — I was *unwilling*. I had said no, and closed myself off from the matter, when all God ever wants, from any of us, is our willingness to be open to the possibility of a yes.

When you really think about it, that's not too much to ask. Being willing doesn't mean we will be required. Perhaps if I had been willing to say yes to what I saw as a need I could address, nothing would have come of it directly, but perhaps indirectly I would have learned something about God, or about myself — or perhaps my children, who are already pretty generous-minded, would have become more generous in action than they already are, which might have shaped their own future paths in unimaginable ways.

We can't know what might have happened, had we taken different paths in our lives. We can't know how a measure of willingness offered up to God, untainted by our willfulness, might have changed a world. But we can recognize that our sins of omission — what we have failed to do — are nothing less than a declaration of unwillingness: a hardy "no" declared unto the Creator, whose whole intention for us is "yes."

A sin of omission is the circle Chesterton talks about. It is a self-enclosure within which we spin, but grow no larger, and into which nothing penetrates. We are all about ourselves, within that circle. To be *willing* is to be open, like the very cross upon which Christ Jesus spread wide his arms. Willingness, like the cross, has width enough for the world, and breadth enough to touch heaven.

—

WHAT DOES CATHOLICISM SAY ABOUT SINS OF OMISSION?

"Amen, I say to you, what you did not do for one
of these least ones, you did not do for me."
— MATTHEW 25:45 (NAB)

"That servant who knew his master's will but did not make
preparations nor act in accord with his will
shall be beaten severely."
— Luke 12:47 (NAB)

So for one who knows the right thing to do and
does not do it, it is a sin.
— James 4:17 (NAB)

There are two causes that lead to sin: either we
do not yet know our duty, or we do not perform
the duty that we know. The former is the sin of
ignorance, the latter of weakness.
— St. Augustine, *Enchiridion on Faith, Hope, and Love*

Three things are necessary for the salvation of man:
to know what he ought to believe; to know what he
ought to desire; and to know what he ought to do.
— St. Thomas Aquinas

Modern man ... has so long believed that right and wrong were only
differences in point of view, that now when evil works itself out in
practice, he is paralyzed to do anything against it.
— Archbishop Fulton J. Sheen

The duties of each moment are the shadows beneath which hides the
divine operation. [...] To escape the distress caused by regret for the
past or fear about the future, this is the rule to follow: leave the past
to the infinite mercy of God, the future to His good Providence, give
the present wholly to His love by being faithful to His grace.
— Jean-Pierre de Caussade, *Abandonment to Divine Providence*

God withholds himself from no one who perseveres.
— St. Teresa of Ávila, *Interior Castle*

HOW DO WE PREVENT OURSELVES
FROM COMMITTING SINS OF OMISSION?

DARE TO BE WILLING: When we have something set before us and our fear kicks in, and with it our unwillingness, we are in danger of saying "no" when we suspect our "yes" is what is required. Sometimes I wonder if it wouldn't help to remember, in these moments, that if the atoms around us cease to move, everything "real" would crumble. Our "reality" is in some ways conceptual: in this form, we are exiles — our truest selves are currently "as unknowable as any distant star" (Chesterton, again). We also know, thanks to quantum theory, that everything that is going on now has always been going on. Everything that is to be has already come.

You'd think, knowing all that, it would be easier to trust, easier to take the leap of faith and be willing.

It is difficult to remember that things are passing, that illusions abound, or even that we are living in exile. But as Christians, we do precisely that. We live in exile to our true home, and to our truest natures, and while we are in this form we must — as Richard John Neuhaus discusses in his book *American Babylon: Notes of a Christian Exile* — maintain a courteous and just citizenship in a world that does not quite understand us or know what to do with us.

And that means daring to be willing.

Heaven knows, none of us are truly worthy of being part of God's creative "yes," but all God ever asks of us is to be willing — and in our willingness, we are privileged to co-create.

That sounds terrifying — really, I know it does. But we need to dare to say "yes" and go on trust; dare to stop protecting ourselves and believe that God will not let us down.

This is what the saints did. Willingness is the stuff of salvation — and not just our salvation but also the whole world's. It took the willingness of many to bring us to where we are today. The Incarnate Word was willing. Mary and Joseph were willing.

Peter and Paul and the martyred apostles were willing. All of the saints were willing. Modern-day exiles — like Cardinal Ignatius Kung Pin Mei, who spent 30 years in Chinese prisons, most of it in solitary confinement — endure great trials because they are simply willing to endure what they must, in order to bear witness to the Truth that is Christ Jesus.

Sure, it's scary. Working amidst the power of Almighty God can never be an enterprise for the fainthearted.

But we need to think about maybe-being-open-to-being-willing to take on what is before us. Our "own" work, again, is God's work. As the angels say, often and often, "Do not be afraid."

PRAY
(THIS PRAYER OR YOUR OWN)

O God, you are certainly a Mystery, and too much for us, too all-encompassing for us to ever know fully in this life. At present, we see, as St. Paul says, "through a glass, darkly" (see 1 Cor 13:12), and our hope is to eventually see you in the full light of heaven, and its radiance. But we know this of you: your whole creation exists because you intend it to exist; you will it to exist; you exhale a continual "yes" to your own intention, and we reside on that air, informed by the Holy Spirit. Help us to imitate your Almighty affirmation, which wills all things, with the affirmations large and small that become for us opportunities to be willing, to be open to your call. We see that nothing grows in "no" — therefore, in action, in prayer, in worship, in rest, in sorrow, in rejoicing, in toil, and in stillness, let our every moment and every breath contain within them components of consent, for we recognize that this is where you reside, and we want to be where you are. In the name of Christ Jesus, second Person of this Holy Triune Mystery, we pray. Amen.

Chapter Thirteen

Self-Recrimination

It is only we who brood over our sins. God does not brood over them; God dumps them at the bottom of the sea.
— St. Benedict of Nursia, attributed

In the last chapter, I admitted — as though it needed saying, if you've read this far — that I am what might be called a champion "*mea culpist*," and this is true, but my instinct toward self-recrimination is less a sign of holiness or spiritual advancement than it is a mere habit (a "little" fault) of thinking that everything is always about me.

This is a function of egoism, of course, but people who have been oft-blamed will tend to be self-conscious, and so their egoism is less about being aggrandized than being afflicted. If they step into a room and things seem tense, they're likely to think, "Oh-oh, what did I do?" They don't exactly look for ways to take blame; they've simply gotten used to thinking that if there is blame to go around, a measure of it is surely to their account.

And that's actually true. We are none of us blameless in life, and 'twas ever thus: "The blame is his who chooses," wrote Plato. "God is blameless." Often, this is a mind-set that seeks heavier penances from their confessors than are really necessary, and that, too, is a function of ego — and yes, it was part of my *modus operandi*.

Then one priest told me he gives exactly the same penance, "One Hail Mary, one Our Father, one Glory Be — in thanksgiving," to every penitent all the time, no matter the sins, because "you know what you've done; you are contrite; if you've come in begging for forgiveness, you've already lived with remorse, and sometimes you've had to work up courage to make a good confession. There are many kinds of penance in all of that. More importantly, God's forgiveness shouldn't feel heavy."

That has come to seem right to me. The desire for heavier penances, which sometimes made me re-confess a sin (because I was certain that a light penance meant my sins really hadn't been heard), had little to do with God and everything to do with *me* and what *I* thought was fitting. But forgiving me is, first, God's job, not mine. And prayers of thanksgiving after receiving mercy seem right, don't they?

Often, I wish priests would spend a little time just talking to us about how our sins affect us. A monk once heard my confession and really *heard* my contrition; he noted how heavily my sin was weighing upon me, and after counseling me very briefly, gave a (very light) penance and then said, "And then, *let this be an end* to this torture you're inflicting upon yourself. If you come to God for mercy, you must trust in it."

I was so grateful. It was a short conversation, but I needed more than to list my sins and go through the form. I needed a priest to really *hear* me, acknowledge my failures, and *respond* to me. Once I knew I had really been heard, I was able, finally, to "let this be an end" and truly trust in God's forgiveness. I could then forgive myself — because if God could forgive me, I'd be an egotistical fool to think I couldn't — and put a bad episode behind me.

Another time, I was ridiculously pleased to have an elderly Chinese priest respond to my confession with a sigh and the words, "Well, *that* was a stupid thing to do" (because I really had done something both stupid and gravely sinful). I was very glad to hear words of mercy only *after* I'd gotten a swift validation that, yeah, there was something stupidly sinful that needed forgiveness, to start with. I knew exactly how badly I'd screwed up, and while the priest's Haiku of Stupidity was agreeable to me ("*You have been stupid / you know you have been stupid / stop being stupid*"). I felt — quite healthily, I think — that a heavy penance really was not needed, in order to pound the lesson home.

Those two confession experiences helped rescue me from a lifelong habit of self-recrimination that had only rendered me maudlin or full of self-hatred, and had too often served as an excuse to afflict my family with a need to — again, and again, and once more, with feeling — give a drama-queening demonstration of the regret that was eating at me. This forced them to reassure me that whatever I'd thought I'd done — whatever I was beating myself up for — it hadn't harmed them half as much as it was harming me.

What an abominable little victim I made of myself, with all of that self-blame that, paradoxically, in the end, kind of made victims of them. I was an emotionally greedy piglet who wanted all of the blame, and all of the consolations too.

There is a kind of idolatry in this: there comes a point where continually beating oneself up becomes an offering to a false godling of the self's ego. "Oh, forsooth! I am too awful for mercy. There is no mercy for one such as me!"

In my earlier book *Strange Gods*, I identify an idol as anything that can be placed between God and oneself, thus cutting off our access to and awareness of the Creator. Overwrought self-recrimination is the ultimate idol: one's own extravagant — dare I say it, flamboyant — remorse and regret is a godling, the idol blocking the route to the reality of the God who invites us to swim in the vast ocean of mercy that is ours for the asking.

Yes, for the mere asking.

Well, why do we need God's mercy, anyway?

We need it because it is honey from the rock; it is the balm that heals all wounds; it is the key that unshackles and the breath of life that rescues us from the small evils that nevertheless stick to us and drag us down, like anchors, into the deep and muddy. We need it because we are creatures who do not understand grace, or forgiveness, enough to routinely look for it in our lives or to help bestow it upon others. We need mercy because it teaches us how to live — not merely how to get through a day, but how to come truly alive within it.

We need mercy because God loves us, waits for us, and pines for us so greatly that he has even turned over judgment to Christ Jesus so that he can be ready for our return, with open arms; so that he can be for us the wayside resting place when we are on the move, and the father ready to kill a fatted calf upon our return.

Like that father, he looks for us. He goes out to meet us when we, like the prodigal son, haven't yet made it fully home. He seeks us out too, when, like the "good son," we are feeling confused and distant; he tries to help us understand, if we will just listen: "You are my beloved child, and everything I have is yours. Trust me, because I formed you, and I love you. I have a plan for you; you may not readily understand at all times, but only trust, and remain in my love."

One could look at a crucifix and argue that trusting and remaining in God's love seems like a sucker's bet, but the saints tell us otherwise. They say that where there is faith, one discovers the triune God who is ever faithful.

And this must be true because, go ahead, look at the crucifix: residing there, in that agony, is the God who knows, the God who is intimately acquainted with all of the mechanisms of pain that have shredded us in our lifetimes. Have we been abused, accused, betrayed, mocked, overworked, exploited, made vulnerable, abandoned, robbed? Yes, so has he, the God who loves us so much that he consented to enter into all of that with us — and to carry our blame, as well — in order that we might, finally, trust in his love for us.

God doesn't especially want our excessive self-recrimination, I don't think. But he clearly wants us to know him. If working through our "little sins" — and accepting a properly balanced measure of blame as part of the cross we must bear — begins the process of our drawing nearer to him, then we shouldn't hesitate:

> We are taught you must blame your father, your sisters, your brothers, the school, the teachers — but never blame yourself. It's never your fault. But it's always your fault, because if you wanted to change you're the one who has got to change. (Katharine Hepburn)

Accepting responsibility for our own actions and choices — for the little sins we discover, when we really look for them — is not the same as wallowing in guilt. In the case of our "little sins," it is really enough to see our faults, acknowledge them, and understand them as the germs and sprouts that will, without attention, become the tares amid our wheat; then we must work to weed them out and be rid of them. Because once we have acknowledged where we are failing, we must try to do better.

That doesn't mean suddenly becoming perfect. None of us are perfect to start with, and if we've set ourselves back with bad habits, we are in for a long journey toward setting ourselves aright. But we are doing well with every foot forward. The merest baby step toward what is holy and good, no matter how small, places us that much further into the power of assent, the co-creative power in which the All-Powerful God meets us.

By amending our behavior, we hope to find release from the myriad self-entrapments that are strangling us in our own garden. We seek to grow in holiness in the garden of God's pleasure, in God's own time.

So, we mustn't overindulge our self-recrimination. Strike the breast three times, do, but then pray for assistance and begin to develop new habits by slowly reshaping the old ones. In this way, we — arduously, and sometimes with setbacks — will become better acquainted with ourselves and more open to seeing (and responding to) God's working in our lives, and in the lives of those around us.

—

WHAT DOES CATHOLICISM SAY ABOUT SELF-RECRIMINATION AND ABOUT MERCY?

Scruples are an infirmity which will make a truce
with a man, but very rarely peace; humility
alone comes off conqueror over them.
— St. Philip Neri

One must erase the word discouragement
from one's dictionary of love.
— St. Elizabeth of the Trinity

Even if Jesus lays on us some part of the Cross, He is there
to help us bear it with self-sacrifice and love.
— Pope St. John XXIII

It is, however ... a laudable and salutary custom to confess all
the venial sins that we remember. But what I wish is that you do not
go too much into detail, be not too punctilious in your accusations.
God does not exact so rigorous an examen. It is that rigor which
exposes you to the loss of liberty and peace of mind, of sweet
and gentle piety of heart.
— St. Peter Julian Eymard

How happy I am to see myself imperfect
and be in need of God's mercy.
— St. Thérèse of Lisieux

My offenses truly I know them;
my sin is always before me.
Against you, you alone, have I sinned;
what is evil in your sight I have done.

That you may be justified when you give sentence
and be without reproach when you judge.
— PSALM 51:3-4

For I do not do the good I want,
but I do the evil I do not want.
— ROMANS 7:19 (NAB)

You have saved me from the pit of destruction,
when you cast behind your back all of my sins.
— SEE ISAIAH 38:17

He will fulfill it if I don't put any obstacle in His way.
— BLESSED TERESA OF CALCUTTA

[A]nd I shall walk in a wide place,
for I have sought your precepts.
I will also speak of your testimonies before kings
and shall not be put to shame,
for I find my delight in your commandments,
which I love.
I will lift up my hands toward your commandments, which I love,
and I will meditate on your statutes.
— PSALM 119:45-48 (ESV)

Q. Why did God make you?
A. God made me to know Him, to love Him, and to serve Him in this
world, and to be happy with Him forever in heaven.
— BALTIMORE CATECHISM

—

HOW DO WE KEEP FROM INDULGING IN SELF-RECRIMINATION?

LET IT GO: As I write this in the Year of Our Lord 2015, I am arguing with a friend for whom every political discussion eventually comes around to 2003, and the Iraqi invasion, which, in hindsight, is easy to call a terrible decision. He wants to keep talking about 2003, and I want to talk about what must be done today, in the circumstances of our time, because what has been done cannot be undone. Rehashing the past is a luxury we cannot afford in the present moment.

He can't let go of it, because he loves having a chance to expound upon what he hates. After a while, hate feels as good as love. I think that's what happens to us too, when we are overindulging in self-recrimination; we love the chance to hate ourselves.

Overindulging in self-recrimination sets us on a loop of self-hatred, over things we have done, and yes, some of them might have been serious sins, but many of them are likely smaller. There is nothing we can do to change the past; we cannot go back in time and re-address our mistakes, missed opportunities, and our dances in the dark. All we can do is go forward — to look at the day before us, and at the present moment we are in, and with a nod to all that has come before, declare, "Knowing what I now know, I will make a better choice, the more loving choice, the less indulgent choice, the less slothful choice." And then make the better choice, in gratitude for your awareness.

GO TO CONFESSION: When you are aware that you are in sin, go get it off your chest, before you start to dwell on it and add elements of drama. If you like, be bold enough to ask for a meaningful penance. I once griped to a confessor that I had spent the whole of one immigrant priest's homily imagining the invention of a microphone that could transform his heavy, indiscernible accent into something I could understand. "I know he's a very holy man," I told my confessor, "but I can't understand a freaking word of his homilies, and I get annoyed." After the pastor explained how heavily he leaned on this priest for his support, I said, "You know what? You should assign me a penance to pray for priests, since I'm complaining so much."

He thought that an excellent idea and agreed. For my penance, I was to pray for all the priests I knew, by name, every morning for a week.

It was a penance, and one involving prayer, but prayer that was neither heavy nor formless. It came to mean a great deal to me, as a privileged duty, performed with and for the Church.

GET OVER YOURSELF: Believe you are forgiven, and that the Sacrament of Reconciliation provides you with extra graces to assist in the avoidance of our stated sins. Otherwise, really, what's the point? You're better than God? He can forgive you, but you can't? Your standards are higher than God's? Oh, friend, get *over* yourself.

DASH IT ALL: When self-recrimination simply will not abate, consider it what the early monks called a "bad thought" and take the advice of St. Benedict, in the third chapter of his Rule: "When evil thoughts come into your heart, dash them at once on the rock of Christ. . . ." It is an amazingly effective mental and spiritual exercise. Just imagine yourself crashing that heavy burden against the cross, just beneath his wounded feet. See how it shatters, and dissipates.

PRAY
(THIS PRAYER OR YOUR OWN)

Lord God, we live in a society that is so superficial, where the word "love," even the concept of love, has been defined downward until we don't really know what is meant by it. We have an idea that we think we know what love is, when we feel it, except that sometimes even hate becomes confused with love, depending upon our emphasis and our interests. Surely, we do not know what you mean when you speak of your love; it is something unimaginable to us and beyond our grasp. Help us to understand love as you have made it manifest, through your word, through your Church, through your sacraments and your Holy Spirit. Help us to seek out your love and, as we absorb it, desire to share it within the day, and the circumstances of it, and to ask for more — more love, more comprehension in our journey toward you — tomorrow. We ask this, as always, in the name of Christ Jesus. Amen.

Conclusion

In the introduction I alluded to the heavy trials I knew I would be inflicting upon my editor, Bert Ghezzi, when he asked me to do this book. The reality is, I really did not want to write it, but I have a terrible time saying no to people I respect, and when they are also charming, as is Bert, I'm pretty helpless.

My reluctance to write it had nothing to do with Bert, but with me.

Have you ever met someone who seems attracted to Christianity, and is always talking about God or asking questions about Scripture, but somehow never gets around to stepping through the church doors? I knew someone like that once, and one day he made it plain why he stayed outside.

"If I go in there," he told me, "I will have to change, and I don't want to."

That's basically my story about this book, in a nutshell. I knew that if I took it on, and started thinking about all the bad habits and "little sins" that are the stuff of my daily existence, I would be forced to confront myself.

I would be forced to change.

Like my cowboy friend, I would have to amend my life and the way I lived it, because Truth would demand it, dammit, and I didn't want to.

Not that I enjoy any part of my sinfulness. I don't. Most especially, I have long been disgusted and unhappy with the concupiscence and gluttony that have kept me entrapped and owned, for decades.

I certainly wanted to change that reality — or, more honestly, I wanted God to change it: just *poof* me into a better me-ness.

Because I believe he loves me, and because I completely believe Christ Jesus when he says in John's Gospel, "Whatever you ask in my name, I will do it, that the Father may be glorified in the Son" (14:13, RSV), that's what I once asked.

Yeah, baby! "Yes, indeedy, Lord! You said it. I believe it. Let's do this thing! *Poof me!*"

I am not a stupid woman, and friends will tell you I am generally pretty swift on the uptake, but it has taken me fully two years to realize that Bert bringing this book to me was my *poof*! As usual, with God, it was a *poof* beyond all understanding, a *poof* that will have to rely on my bare understanding of quantum theory in order to see two stagnant years as a "*poof*"!

It was the answer to a prayer uttered so often in good faith: "Lord, help me to be better; help me to be a better person, a better wife and mother, a better friend, a better boss, a better human, a better creature, a better me! Because I hates me. Come on, Lord ... *please*?"

But I've always known I would have to just do the work — that my spiritual life would not be best served by just "*poofing*" anything. God could certainly do it, but it wouldn't be good for me. I knew it wouldn't be good for me, any more than "simple" surgical solutions (that seem like cheating) would be good for me — because I know myself, and how deeply ungrateful I usually am. Jesus had to carry his cross, and not *poof* himself down from it, and I have to carry mine with the same laborious obedience he has modeled for us, because that will give my change in habits meaning. The changes I make will help to heal my spirit in places where the wounds are deep.

So, writing this has been a toothache of a process, mostly because it turned into — as I had predicted it would — a kind of mini-memoir, whereby I have been forced to confront myself (ugh!), but it has always been self-revelatory in very constructive ways. Typing out the fact that I've allowed regret to eat at me was a lightbulb moment — as was the idea of swallowing anger, choking back words.

Ugh, ugh, I have so much work to do! It is making me anxious, because when you write a book like this, knowing full well that you are the walking embodiment of all of these bad habits and sins, you know the first thing the world is going to do when it is released is take a good hard look at the author and say, "Physician, heal thy awful self," and "Seriously? You wrote this book?"

I finish this effort, therefore, on a bittersweet note: writing it has been helpful. "You have shown me the path of life," if I really want to live what is left of it, and asking for do-overs is not an option.

Now, I have to actually live the book I have written. I must re-read all of those practical suggestions at the end of each chapter and, if I am not already taking them myself, finally begin to integrate them into my life.

But I want to, now. Finally, I want to take on the *poof* God is offering me, instead of the one I had goofily imagined. Because God never sells us short. He never takes the cheap and easy route, either, because cheap and easy usually means a crummy gift, and we are promised an extravagance of riches, if we are only faithful, and paying attention.

It bears repeating:

A voice I did not know said to me:
"I freed your shoulder from the burden;
your hands were freed from the load.
You called in distress and I saved you.

I answered, concealed in the storm cloud;
at the waters of Meribah I tested you.
Listen, my people, to my warning.
O Israel, if only you would heed!

Let there be no foreign god among you.
no worship of an alien god.
I am the Lord your God,
who brought you from the land of Egypt.
Open wide your mouth and I will fill it." (Ps 81:6b-11)

If I sound excited, it's only because I am. How could I not be: I am on a great adventure with a God who wants to lavish me with gifts, if I will only pay attention. I believe this. I know it is true. And it is true for all of us.

Please pray for me.

NOTES

1. St. Thomas Aquinas, *STh* II-II, 64, 7, *corp. art.*
2. "Christians must resist 'dark joy' of gossiping, pope says," Catholic News Service (March 27, 2013); http://www.catholicnews.com /services/englishnews/2013/christians-must-resist-dark-joy-of -gossiping-pope-says.cfm.
3. Cf. CIC, can. 220.
4. Cf. Sir 21:28.
5. "Pope: There is no such thing as innocent gossip," News.va (Sept. 13, 2013); http://www.news.va/en/news/pope-there-is-no-such -thing-as-innocent-gossip.
6. St. Ignatius of Loyola, *Spiritual Exercises*, 22.
7. Jas 4:3; cf. the whole context: Jas 4:1-10; 1:5-8; 5:16.
8. Jas 4:4.
9. Jas 4:5.
10. Evagrius Ponticus, *De oratione* 34: PG 79, 1173.
11. St. Augustine, *Ep.* 130, 8, 17:PL 33, 500.
12. A portion of the following originally appeared as an essay ("May Anger Begin to Abate with Gratitude?") in *First Things* (July 10, 2012, online); http://www.firstthings.com/web -exclusives/2012/07/may-anger-begin-to-abate-with-gratitude.
13. St. Nicholas of Flüe; cf. Mt 5:29-30; 16:24-26.
14. Pope Benedict XVI, *The God of Jesus Christ: Meditations on the Triune God* (San Francisco: Ignatius Press, 2008), 53-54.
15. Henri J. M. Nouwen, *Bread for the Journey: A Daybook of Wisdom and Faith* (New York: HarperCollins, 1997), 59.
16. Elizabeth Scalia, "The Value of Conscience," *The Catholic Answer* (May/June 2012), 38; https://www.osv.com/OSVNewsweekly /ByIssue/Article/TabId/735/ArtMID/13636/ArticleID/9796/The -Value-of-Conscience.aspx.
17. Cf. Deut 25:13-16; 24:14-15; Jas 5:4; Am 8:4-6.